'This book analyses recent developments in the evolution of news culture. It provides an insightful picture of the changing dynamics between PR and journalism, highlighting the challenges these developments pose to social justice and democracy. Underpinned by strong empirical research and theorising, this is brilliant and very important book!'

Maureen McNeil, Professor Emerita, Department of Sociology, Lancaster University, UK

I0123770

Secrecy in Public Relations, Mediation and News Cultures

This book investigates the relationship of secrecy as a social practice to contemporary media, news cultures and public relations.

Drawing on Georg Simmel's theorisation of how secrecy produces a 'second world' alongside the 'obvious world' and creates and reshapes social relations, Anne Cronin argues for close analysis of the PR industry as a powerful vector of secrecy and an examination of its relationship to news cultures. Using case studies and in-depth interviews, as well as recent research in media and cultural studies, sociology, journalism studies and communication studies, the book analyses how PR practices generate a second, shadow world of the media sphere which has a profound impact on the 'obvious world'. It interrogates both the PR industry's and news culture's role in shaping social relations for a digital media landscape, and those initiatives promoting transparency of data and decision-making processes.

An insightful, interdisciplinary approach to debates on media and power, this book will appeal to students of public relations, sociology, media studies, cultural studies and communication studies. It will also be of interest to scholars and practitioners working at the intersections of media, social relations and public trust.

Anne M. Cronin is Professor of Cultural Sociology at Lancaster University, UK. Her previous books include *Public Relations Capitalism: Promotional Culture, Publics and Commercial Democracy* (2018); *Advertising, Commercial Spaces and the Urban* (2010); *Advertising Myths: The Strange Half-Lives of Images and Commodities* (2004); *Advertising and Consumer Citizenship: Gender, Images and Rights* (2000).

Routledge Focus on Media and Cultural Studies

For more information about this series, please visit: https://www.routledge.com/Routledge-Focus-on-Media-and-Cultural-Studies/book-series/RFMCS

Secrecy in Public Relations, Mediation and News Cultures

The Shadow World of the Media Sphere

Anne M. Cronin

Routledge
Taylor & Francis Group

LONDON AND NEW YORK

First published 2023
by Routledge
4 Park Square, Milton Park, Abingdon, Oxon OX14 4RN

and by Routledge
605 Third Avenue, New York, NY 10158

Routledge is an imprint of the Taylor & Francis Group, an informa business

British Library Cataloguing-in-Publication Data
A catalogue record for this book is available from the British Library

ISBN: 978-1-032-43410-0 (hbk)
ISBN: 978-1-032-43955-6 (pbk)
ISBN: 978-1-003-36958-5 (ebk)

DOI: 10.4324/9781003369585

Typeset in Times New Roman
by codeMantra

Contents

Acknowledgements

My thanks to the Leverhulme Trust which supported this research with a Research Fellowship (RF-2021-001). I am grateful to all the participants of this study who gave up time to be interviewed. Many thanks also to the various people who have helped me think through the ideas for this book: Lee Edwards, Anne-Marie Fortier, Hilary Hinds, Maureen McNeil, Paul Newnham and Cindy Weber. Thanks also to the editorial team at Routledge.

1   Introduction

Secrets are powerfully appealing. They pique our interest and tap into our curiosity. They have a magnetism which paradoxically pulls in two directions: secrets want to be kept (they maintain their allure and power by not being divulged), but secrets also want to be shared, told and revealed. This hints at secrecy's socially embedded character. Studies show that secrecy is a compelling social force, organising power relations and actively structuring social relations at a profound level. In this way, secrecy mediates social relations, and the media are the prime means through which secrets are revealed and widely circulated. It is, therefore, surprising that there have been so few studies of secrecy and the media. Media analysis tends to focus on *that which is represented* and how it is framed – the content of news reports, social media feeds and television programmes.[1] But there is less focus on that which is intentionally concealed.[2]

This book analyses the relationship between secrecy and what Simmel (1906) called 'publicity' – the making public of issues, interests, practices, relations, etc. I frame this relationship throughout the book as the secrecy–publicity dynamic. I take as my focus the UK public relations (PR) industry (specifically media relations PR) and its interface with journalism and news media. PR operates at the fulcrum of the secrecy–publicity dynamic: one of PR's core aims is to obscure or downplay negative issues relating to its clients, while another is to gain for them as much positive publicity as possible. All the while, PR attempts to remain 'the unseen power' (Cutlip 1994) executed by what Bernays (2005 [1928]: 37) calls 'invisible governors', obscuring the role the PR industry plays in influencing media content and in shaping the very practices which structure publicity today. This book also analyses the place of journalism and news media in the secrecy–publicity dynamic and assesses their relationship to PR. Journalism is clearly

DOI: 10.4324/9781003369585-1

engaged in investigating and revealing issues of public interest, but it also has a complex and shifting relationship to secrecy.

While I cannot hope to reveal specific secrets – although I do relay the intriguing secrecy practices I encountered in my research with PR practitioners and journalists – throughout this book I gather and analyse material with the aim of revealing the *shape* of secrets and how secrecy is engineered. I show how secrecy practices are active in making social relations and shaping society, and analyse how practices of secrecy interface with practices of publicity. I argue that secrecy practices contribute to making 'a shadow world of the media sphere' and assess the significance of this for society in general. While there are specificities relating to the UK's media and legal systems, my conceptual framing of the dynamics of secrecy and publicity offers an important starting point for analysing other national media contexts. Further, my analysis demonstrates how PR's techniques of secrecy, and use of technologies such as social media, transcend national boundaries and act to reshape social relations.

The empirical research on which this book is based consists of 40 in-depth, semi-structured interviews with UK public relations practitioners, journalists, news editors, representatives of PR industry trade bodies, and representatives of organisations interested in transparency over the period 2020–2021. Participants were offered the option of being named or remaining anonymous. In the latter case I also anonymised any details which may identify them such as employer or specific cases they discussed. The interview material was transcribed and coded using Atlas.ti qualitative data software. This material provided fascinating insights which I have supplemented with an analysis of case studies and various examples. The addition of ethnographic data would have further enriched the analysis, but such access is unsurprisingly difficult to secure when issues of secrecy are at play (see Sheaff 2019). Nevertheless, I believe my analysis offers new empirical insights and new conceptual framings that will benefit studies of PR, news cultures, journalism and media and secrecy.

Chapter 2 outlines existing debates about secrecy and explores their intersection with debates about PR and news media. I introduce Simmel's (1906) work on secrecy and discuss how I have adapted it to analyse what I term 'the shadow world of the media sphere'. Drawing on my empirical data, Chapter 3 discusses PR's techniques of secrecy and publicity, such as distraction and diversion, 'data bombing' or 'snowing', 'astroturfing' and the creation of counterfeit news stories, pre-emptive measures and 'preventive revelations', the use of expert opinion and the role of 'product defence companies'. Chapter 4 analyses how the secrecy–publicity dynamic operates in journalism and news cultures – and their intersection with PR – and I examine Non-Disclosure Agreements (NDAs) and DSMA-Notices as key 'social technologies of secrecy'. Chapter 5 extends this analysis by considering modes of revelation such as Freedom of Information (FOI) requests, leaks and whistleblowing in news cultures and the shaping of information release in PR through narrative techniques. Chapter 6 draws together the arguments of the book and extends them to consider not only the production and influence of the shadow world of the media sphere but also the ways in which the very meanings and social freight of secrecy and publicity may be changing.

Notes

1 There is a parallel focus on that which is *excluded* from media representation and media industries such as various social groups (the disabled, racialised groups, etc.), but exclusion has a rather different valence from concealment and secrecy.
2 Although, as I discuss in later chapters, some studies of journalism examine practices of secrecy such as state secrecy.

References

Bernays, E. (2005 [1928]) *Propaganda*. Brooklyn, NY: Ig Publishing.
Cutlip, S. M. (1994) *The Unseen Power: Public Relations. A History*. Hillsdale, NJ: Lawrence Erlbaum Associates.
Sheaff, M. (2019) *Secrecy, Privacy and Accountability: Challenges for Social Research*. Cham: Palgrave Macmillan.
Simmel, G. (1906) 'The sociology of secrecy and of secret societies', *American Journal of Sociology*, 11(4): 441–498.

2 Framing secrecy, publicity and news media cultures

In this chapter, I outline some of the key debates about secrecy, public relations and journalism and news media cultures. There are extensive and wide-ranging discussions in the fields of both PR and of journalism and news media cultures, but my focus is restricted to their specific points of intersection. More particularly, I am interested in their relationship as seen through the lens of secrecy and secrecy's interface with what Simmel (1906: 469) has termed 'publicity', including one of its key manifestations today – 'transparency'.

Conceptualising secrecy

Secrecy has been examined from the disciplinary perspectives of anthropology, sociology, philosophy, history, politics, literary studies and media studies, among others. Although its precise characterisation varies from study to study – inflected with the emphasis associated with each discipline – secrecy's defining trait is generally understood to be 'consciously willed concealment' (Simmel 1906: 449; see also Bok 1989). The most influential study of secrecy as a socially embedded practice is that of Georg Simmel (1906). Simmel is generally understood to have been a sociologist although critics have noted, 'his ability to range across academic disciplines' (Featherstone 1991: 2). This generosity of disciplinary approach in his thinking has sometimes been understood and critiqued as a 'pluralistic-unsystematic tendency' (Lukács 1991: 147), although, more positively, some have remarked on his 'boundless and unrestrained sensibility' and 'his joy at the qualitative and the unique' (Lukács 1991: 146, 148). Simmel was interested in the everyday and the ways in which ordinary, interpersonal and often routine practices contribute to the constitution of societies (Frisby 1986, 1992). Focusing on how social relations were created through interaction and relationality, Simmel wanted to avoid reifying 'society' as a concept: 'Simmel's conceptions of society are

DOI: 10.4324/9781003369585-2

either directly grounded in or presuppose the concept of interaction or reciprocal effect (*Wechselwirkung*)' (Frisby 1992: 7). The dynamism of interaction and the significance of the relational were key in his work, including that focusing on secrecy. Simmel offers a nuanced analytic framework that can capture the mutual influence of multiple elements while also accounting for change.

Georg Simmel (1906) argued that secrecy is present in all societies as an animating force that actively constitutes those societies. In this sense, secrecy is *productive* of social relations rather than simply acting as a containing or repressive force. As a means of constituting social relations, Simmel emphasised that the form and social practices of secrecy are in themselves morally neutral: 'Secrecy is a universal sociological form, which, as such, has nothing to do with the moral valuations of its contents' (1906: 463). It is of such social significance that Simmel understood secrecy as a foundational characteristic of humans and their relationship with one another, and as a capacity that extends human achievements and potential:

> Secrecy in this sense – i.e., which is effective through negative or positive means of concealment – is one of the greatest accomplishments of humanity. In contrast with the juvenile condition in which every mental picture is at once revealed, every undertaking is open to everyone's view, secrecy procures enormous extension of life, because with publicity many sorts of purposes could never arrive at realization... Every relationship between two individuals or two groups will be characterized by the ratio of secrecy that is involved in it.
>
> Simmel (1906: 462)

Secrecy can be contrasted with what Simmel (1906: 469) terms 'publicity' – the making public or making known – of information, interests or relationships. Secrecy is, thus, a practice, form and social relationship. It is highly compelling and its appeal for individuals and groups, Simmel suggests, derives from its form and dynamics rather than the content of any particular secret. Simmel (1906: 464) discusses how the 'peculiar attraction' of secrecy originates from several sources: secrecy offers the appeal of exclusivity in the possession of the secret (as an individual or part of a group which is 'in on the secret'), while offering the satisfaction of knowing that others are excluded from that knowledge and from that restricted group:

> ...the strongly accentuated exclusion of all not within the circle of secrecy results in a correspondingly accentuated feeling of personal possession. For many natures possession acquires its

proper significance, not from the mere fact of having, but besides that there must be the consciousness that others must forgo the possession.

Simmel (1906: 464)

The practice of secrecy also generates an aura and thus a sense of enhanced value in which 'that what is withheld from the many appears to have special value' (Simmel 1906: 464). This aura can relate to the contents of a particular secret or a person associated with the secret: 'Secrecy gives the person enshrouded by it an exceptional position' (Simmel 1906: 464). The productive character of secrecy is evident here: the creation of aura through secrecy fosters and shapes social relations in the light of such perceptions of value.

For Simmel, secrecy exists in a dynamic tension with publicity (the making public or rendering visible of information, interests, relationships, etc.). The power of the secret originates not only from its capacity to create exclusive groups with restricted knowledge, but from the tension inherent in the constant threat of exposure of the secret and in the appeal of passing on the secret to others outside the group. In this way, 'the possibility and the temptation of treachery plays around the secret' (Simmel 1906: 466). Thus, secrecy practices create social groups oriented around secrets while also setting into play powerful counter forces oriented by the magnetic appeal of unveiling those secrets (and dissolving the special character of the group holding those secrets):

> Secrecy sets barriers between men, but at the same time offers the seductive temptation to break through the barriers by gossip or confession. This temptation accompanies the psychical life of the secret like an overtone.... Secrecy involves a tension which, at the moment of revelation, finds its release.
>
> . Simmel (1906: 466, 465)

This highlights Simmel's interest in the reciprocal character of social relations and the generative quality of relationality. The dynamic tensions that exist between secrecy and publicity in varying proportions, and with varying character according to time and place, are emblematic of Simmel's focus on the significance of the relational: 'From the play of these two interests, in concealment and in revelation, spring shadings and fortunes of human reciprocities throughout their whole range' (Simmel 1906: 466).

Simmel's intriguing work on secrecy opened up new dimensions of social relationships for examination, framing those dimensions as a 'second world'. In claiming that 'secrecy procures enormous extension of life', Simmel highlighted secrecy's capacity to conceal intentions and provide a protected, obscured space in which individuals and groups can plan and strategise distanced from the gaze of others: 'Secrecy secures, so to speak, the possibility of a second world alongside of the obvious world, and the latter is most strenuously affected by the former' (Simmel 1906: 462). I elaborate throughout the book how this 'second world', or what I am calling the 'shadow world' of the media sphere, is shaped by practices of both secrecy and publicity in PR and news media cultures, and, in turn, influences today's manifestations of secrecy and publicity throughout society more generally.

More recent accounts have drawn on Simmel's insights about the creative powers of secrecy in order to analyse a range of contexts and disciplinary concerns. In sociology, the socially embedded character of secrecy and its capacity to create social relations have been explored in a number of ways, for instance, in how the keeping and revealing of secrets can constitute and reconfigure families (Smart 2011) and can mediate stigma over generations (Barnwell 2019). Anthropology has long had an interest in both secrecy and secret societies or collectives, exploring how secrecy creates social connections, boundaries, groups and norms (see Herdt 1990; Jones 2014; Taussig 1999). In relation to narrative and secrecy, I examine anthropological accounts of 'myth' as stories which act to constitute social formations in Chapter 5. Literary accounts have provided subtle analyses of how fiction can provide a space for readers to explore the tensions that secrecy establishes in society. Melley's (2012) account of secrecy analyses how fiction can provide a space for the American public to imagine and fantasise about U.S. foreign policy, presenting and resolving certain contradictions and tensions.[1] This fiction, and readers' engagement with it, creates what Melley (2012: 5–6) terms 'the covert sphere' which is,

[a] cultural imaginary shaped by both institutional secrecy and public fascination with the secret work of the state.... Through a combination of state secrecy and public representation, the covert sphere not only smooths over the central contradiction of the Cold War state — that Western democracy can preserve itself only through the suspension of democracy—but it turns this troubling proposition into a source of public reassurance and even pleasure.

Melley (2012: 5–6)

The very form and structure of fiction, as well as its freedom from legal strictures, may offer a unique site though which to stage and explore secrecy. As Eva Horn argues,

> Secrets generate conjectures; they trigger narratives designed to make sense of events that are removed from knowledge. When we are unable (or unqualified) to know what 'really' happened, the only thing left to do is to construct plausible versions.... Fictions illuminate secrecy's structure because they reconstruct its logic, its subtle and mysterious economy of light and dark, truth and lies, presence and absence. Unlike memoirs or historical accounts, fiction is able to circumvent the legal interdictions that necessarily surround state secrets, whether gag orders and secrecy clauses imposed on insiders or the classification of certain types of information. 'Invention' has always been a mask to reveal otherwise unspeakable truths. But the main reason for fiction's lucidity lies in its poetic structure: through the form of its narrative, its subtle play of allusion and mysteriousness, implication and explication, the literary narrative can make the secret 'readable', decipherable without explicitly solving it, thereby rendering visible the structure of a type of knowledge inextricably entangled with non-knowledge, truth blended with lie.
>
> Horn (2013: 25)

Literary accounts explore secrecy's dynamics by inhabiting and manipulating secrecy's own form, and I explore in later chapters how understandings of narrative, located within broader discursive formations, can illuminate how secrecy and its relationship to publicity operate in the communications produced by both PR and journalism.

A common thread that runs through analyses of secrecy from various disciplines is a sensitivity to secrecy's interface with power and power relations. While it is clear that secrecy is not only a strategy of the powerful, as it can be mobilised by less powerful groups or insurgent or revolutionary movements (Birchall 2021), secrecy's relationship to the powerful is historically very well established. One strand of analysis explores the relationship between secrecy, the state and power. In her discussion of secret societies and totalitarian movements, Hannah Arendt (1951: 386) notes that 'real power begins where secrecy begins'. Historical studies have explored how secrecy develops unevenly alongside ideas of privacy and 'publicity' (Vincent 1998), and that different logics of secrecy in politics develop over time (Foucault 2007; Horn 2011). Security studies have paid close attention to secrecy, for instance, tracing what Masco (2010: 440, 441) terms 'the political deployment of the secret as idea', in which the national security state is oriented by 'the theatrical performance of secrecy as a means to power: secrecy now functions as a form of antiknowledge, an empty signifier that stands in for governance, rationality, and evidence'. Studies note that secrecy at the level of the state is difficult to accomplish and its practice fosters an intense public curiosity about what may be hidden and the means by which such information is hidden (Fenster 2014), while other studies focus on the textual or rhetorical means by which state secrecy, alongside disclosure or leaking, may be practiced (Bail 2015; Lefebvre 2021).

Another strand of research examines the relationship between secrecy, capitalism and power, although secrecy is rarely the primary focus. Max Weber (1997), for example, notes the role of secrecy in supporting bureaucracy and the dominant power structures of society.

> Every bureaucracy seeks to increase the superiority of the professionally informed by keeping their knowledge and intentions secret. Bureaucratic administration always tends to be an administration of 'secret sessions': in so far as it can, it hides its knowledge and action from criticism.... The tendency toward secrecy in certain administrative fields follows their material nature: everywhere that the power interests of the domination structure toward *the outside* are at stake, whether it is an economic competitor of a private enterprise, or a foreign, potentially hostile polity, we find secrecy.
>
> Weber (1997: 233, original emphasis)

Weber's insights have been developed by Costas and Grey (2016: 141) who analyse how secrecy is the 'hidden architecture' of organisations: secrecy is both embedded in and acts to constitute organisations. This takes various forms including 'formal secrecy' (such as trade secrets), which are 'officially sanctioned and organized through prescriptive rules or laws', and 'informal secrecy', such as, 'confidential gossip, which operate unofficially and are organized through social norms' (Costas & Grey 2016: 8).[2]

Secrecy and concealment are also central elements in Karl Marx's (1990) account of commodity fetishism. Marx (1990: 164) wrote of 'the mysterious character of the commodity-form' in which the human labour involved in making the commodity comes to be concealed and instead reappears as if it were a natural characteristic of the commodity. The only true value of a commodity, according to Marx, derives from the labour that has been expended in producing it. But under a system of capitalism, this process is hidden and commodities appear to gain independent value that is calibrated against other commodities rather than the labour power of the workers who produced them. 'The determination of the magnitude of value by labour-time is therefore a secret hidden under the apparent movements in the relative values of commodities' (Marx 1990: 168). The commodity as a product of labour is transformed into 'a social hieroglyphic' and 'men try to decipher the hieroglyphic, to get behind the secret of their own social product' (Marx 1990: 167). In a related analysis, Georg Simmel (2004: 385) argues that secrecy and the money form are intimately intertwined as money makes possible, 'the secrecy, invisibility and silence of exchange'.[3]

Marx's work, in turn, inspired later accounts which examine the relationship between capitalism, concealment and secrecy. Guy Debord's (1995: 12) account of 'the society of the spectacle' as 'a social relationship between people that is mediated by images' in a market society was based on an analysis of visuality. In a later discussion of this work, he argues that concealment and secrecy are key elements of the society of the spectacle: 'Generalised secrecy stands behind the spectacle, as the decisive complement of all it displays and, in the last analysis, as its most vital operation' (Debord 1998: 12). Capitalism's structure and ideologies are established and maintained by '"front" organisations' such as advertising which 'draw an impenetrable screen over the concentrated wealth of their members' (Debord 1998: 52). The veiling of the operation and the true nature of capitalist social relations are secured by practices of secrecy which aide in social forgetting: 'With consummate skill the spectacle organises ignorance of what is about to happen and, immediately afterwards, the forgetting of whatever has nonetheless been understood. The more important something is, the more it is hidden' (Debord 1998: 14).

Jodi Dean (2002) has produced a fascinating and influential analysis of the relationship between secrecy and publicity, the exploration of which is intertwined with the account of 'communicative capitalism' developed throughout her work (Dean 2005, 2009, 2019). Dean (2002) argues that the proliferation of communication technologies and the huge flux of messages and images they facilitate do not foster enhanced democracy as some may imagine, but rather instantiate and support a form of capitalism that feeds off information to bolster capital accumulation. The internet and communication technologies promise freedom, but these are only the freedoms of the market. Instead of supporting the potential for genuine democratic engagement and political change, 'the deluge of screens and spectacles undermines political opportunity and efficacy for most of the world's peoples' (Dean 2002: 3). Dean argues that in communicative capitalism, meaning has been occluded and the value of communication comes to reside primarily in its circulation and, more precisely, how that circulation can be monetised: 'the exchange value of messages overtakes their use value... the message is simply part of a circulating data stream. Its particular content is irrelevant' (2005: 58). As meaning becomes emptied out, the affective dimension of communication comes to prominence, an effect 'which is most powerful when it contains different, conflicting meanings' (Dean 2019: 332). In this way, the power of messages derives from their capacity to elicit an affective response such as outrage or amusement (Dean 2019), so evident in the patterns of messaging on social media.

Dean's (2002) understanding of the relationship between secrecy and publicity is situated within this broader account of communicative capitalism. She argues that the abundance of information circulating in today's communicative capitalism has at its core a paradox: 'at just the moment when everything seems fully public, the media pulses with invocations of the secret' (2002: 1). Such a technoculture promises democracy through publicity – making everything public. Indeed, 'publicity and secrecy provide the matrix through which we think about democracy and within which technoculture is materialized.... Publicity is what makes today's communicative capitalism seem perfectly natural' (Dean 2002: 4). Publicity functions as the ideology of technoculture, helping consolidate wealth and power in corporations, and publicity instantiates a general principle of access to information: 'everyone has a right to know' (Dean 2002: 151). Alongside this sense that everything is fully exposed in a supposedly democratic public sphere that is facilitated by communication technologies, there is a parallel sense that secrets abound. Communicative capitalism fosters a public perception that there is always more to be uncovered and that the answers are 'out there', requiring only more intense deployment of communication technologies to discover them. This, Dean (2002) argues, binds us more tightly to the market of communications technologies created by capitalism. In turn, this feeds into conspiracy thinking: that things are not as they seem, that everything is connected and that there are shadowy elites in control behind the scenes. Indeed, Dean (2002: 12) argues that 'the democratic subject today is interpellated as a conspiring subject'.[4] We are incited to engage in a never-ending, compulsive search for information, thus invoking 'the secret as a hidden object of desire' (Dean 2002: 12). Technoculture fascinates us and communication technologies become the fetish that seems to offer us the means of uncovering secrets and unveiling the promised answers. But an ever-more intensive engagement with technoculture merely consolidates the power of communicative capitalism and, in parallel, forecloses politics by deferring action: 'Action is postponed until a thorough study is undertaken, until all the facts are known' (Dean 2002: 163). Of course, communicative capitalism figures the search for information as unending, thus paralysing political action in Dean's view. In effect, 'in contemporary technoculture, a dynamic of publicity and secrecy hurts rather than helps democracy. It produces communicative capitalism as the lure of secrets, and the promise of revelation circulates throughout cyberia's networks' (Dean 2002: 81).

Dean's argument draws on Žižek's (1989) work and on Derrida's (1994) account of the 'secrecy effect' or the dynamic of knowing and speculation: 'Wherever knowledge can only be supposed, wherever, as a result, one knows that supposition cannot give rise to knowledge, wherever no knowledge could ever be disputed, there is the production of a secrecy effect, of what we might be able to call a speculation on the capital secret or on the capital of the secret' (Derrida 1994: 245). In addition, Dean's account of the dynamic tension that exists between secrecy and publicity clearly owes a great deal to Simmel's work. But while her analysis offers some intriguing insights, it operates at a high level of generality that does not do justice to the complex patterning and nuances of communication practices and technologies under capitalism, or the socially embedded character of secrecy practices and their relationship to publicity that so interested Simmel. Her claim that the meanings of communications have become erased at the expense of circulation does not bear close scrutiny, as we can see, for instance, from the range of ways that activists use communications to leverage their goals (for example, see Boyle 2019; Demetrious 2013, 2019; Mundt et al. 2018; Poell 2014). Her point, following Simmel, that the relationship between secrecy and publicity is central in today's societies is important, but she pays little attention to the specificities of how they are enacted and, indeed, challenged, instead building her argument on detailed theoretical discussion which is compelling yet ungrounded. Dean's theoretical framing is itself seductive: it presents itself as an academic power tool that, ironically, seems to promise full intelligibility of the system of capitalism. But, theoretical seductions can distract from societies' messy material power relations and can gloss over how capitalism is made, unmade and remade in shifting ways that are impossible to capture as neatly as some theories may suggest. As Gibson-Graham (1996, 2006) point out, there is a risk of framing capitalism in such a way that both naturalises it and renders the ways of challenging capitalist practices less visible.

My account focuses on the materialities, discursive framings, power relations and institutional and legal infrastructures relating to media relations PR practice and its relation to journalism and news media cultures through the analytic entry point of secrecy. As Simmel (1906) argues, the relationship between secrecy and 'publicity' (as a mode of 'making public') is dynamic and one of the most dominant forms of publicity in today's democratic societies, I suggest, is 'transparency'.

Publicity as transparency

The principle of transparency that is being implemented across many organisations and societal forms such as governmental bodies and corporations promotes openness in terms of access to information and public understanding of procedures and practices. Transparency has gained considerable traction in many democratic societies: 'It is an apparently simple solution to complex problems – such as how to fight corruption, promote trust in government, support corporate social responsibility, and foster state accountability' (Birchall 2014: 77). But transparency practices are far from being simple and efficient means of mobilising the democratic principle of rendering issues visible to the public (Birchall 2021; Brighenti 2007; Schudson 2020). As Etzioni (2010) argues, there tends to be an over-valuing of transparency and its potential. The complexity or specialised nature of certain forms of information means that simply releasing that information may not translate into a public understanding of it or an appreciation of its significance. Reliance is, therefore, placed on intermediaries such as journalists to interpret information for the public, but this raises questions about how those intermediaries are regulated (Etzioni 2010). Furthermore, far from being a neutral principle or practice, transparency is itself shot through with power relations and is freighted with ideological weight. This is evident, for instance, in the promotion of transparency measures oriented by particular political goals: 'ideological advocates of transparency maintain that it can obviate the need for most – if not all – government controls. That is, transparency becomes a tool to fight off the regulations opposed by various business groups and politicians from conservative parties' (Etzioni, 2010: 390). As Birchall (2016) notes, alongside fending off regulatory controls, transparency measures can transfer responsibility for monitoring and regulation from the state to the citizen: by placing information in the public realm, the state can claim that principles of democratic openness are upheld while divesting responsibility to the public for auditing and holding to account official bodies and corporations. Indeed, transparency measures can simply make inequitable systems operate more efficiently and act to benefit and consolidate the market (Birchall 2014, 2016). On a broader scale, the impact of transparency measures can actively reshape social relations: 'As a form of management or governance, transparency *reconfigures* – rather than *reproduces* – its objects and subjects' (Flyverbom 2016: 112), enacting change in ways that may be strategic or unintentional.

Transparency practices tend to take the form of one-way communication rather than engaging more democratic principles of dialogue. As Moore (2018) argues, the transparency principle of open government is often understood as a condition achieved by the state through its actions (such as releasing data), rather than by a two-way dialogue or relationship between a state and its citizens as active participants. Further, transparency practices feed into the dynamic tension between secrecy–publicity that Simmel (1906) described. Drawing on Shilling and Mellor's (2015) point that organisations today are perceived by the public to be prone to duplicity, and that the reality is hidden somewhere backstage, Moore argues that transparency practices may simply fuel distrust: 'Transparency, in this context, is more likely to frustrate than assuage concerns about doubleness, not least of all because it expressly denies the possibility that anything is being hidden' (2018: 424). The interrelationship of secrecy and publicity (here manifest as transparency) is evident, one providing definitional shape to the other. As Birchall (2014) notes, the perceived value of transparency as a principle and practice derives from that which it avoids, such as secrecy, but also other forms of 'informal', negatively inflected disclosure such as gossip.

In the context of understanding transparency practices as ideological and power-laden, their role in certain contexts can be framed as a form of 'visibility management' (Flyverbom 2016: 111). Transparency here functions less as democratic openness than as a means of shaping public perceptions. Flyverbom notes that mediating technologies have 'distinct organizing properties that shape what comes to be presented as transparent' (2016: 111), which alerts us to the specificities of mediation, for example, social media posts or reports placed on corporate web sites. But it also, I suggest, highlights the importance of analysing the specificities of certain intermediary roles such as public relations in shaping transparency.

The UK PR industry and its relationship to news media cultures

The occupational category of public relations encompasses a wide range of specialisms such as events management and crisis management, but as the focus of this book is secrecy in the news media sphere and its mediation by public relations, my discussion of PR literature is largely restricted to the specialism of media relations PR. PR or strategic communications can be understood as a form of interest-driven or persuasive communication and includes the management of relationships with a client's publics, which might be the general public, stakeholders and potential stakeholders, regulatory bodies and so on (for an overview of the industry, see Edwards 2018; Moloney & McGrath 2020; Tench & Yeomans 2009). The PR specialism of media relations deals with media (including mainstream media such as television and print media, as well as other forms such as social media), and centres on contacting and courting journalists, producing press releases and other material for dissemination, shaping communications, monitoring and supporting client reputation and managing a range of communications channels including social media feeds.[5]

Assessments of the size of the UK PR industry vary considerably. The Public Relations and Communications Association (PRCA) estimated that there were 97,300 practitioners employed in the industry in 2020, although the Covid-19 pandemic appeared to be prompting redundancies (PRCA 2020). According to the Chartered Institute of Public Relations (CIPR), of the respondents in its annual survey, 45% had worked in the media (such as journalism or publishing) prior to entering the PR industry (CIPR 2020). As many of the participants in this study reported, this represents a long-established trend in which many journalists leave the field of journalism in order to work in the PR industry in search of better pay, conditions and career progression (see also my previous study, Cronin 2018). A background in journalism benefits PR practitioners as they are familiar with the field of media and its practices, they recognise which stories or angles on stories may appeal to journalists and they know how to shape a press release or other PR material in a way which increases its chance of being picked up and reported.

Although there are very few dedicated studies of PR in social science and media and cultural studies research (in contrast to communication studies), many classic analyses make passing reference to PR. C. Wright Mills (1959), for instance, points to PR's role in manipulating the public. Habermas (1991) frames PR, or 'opinion management', as a form of manipulation which detrimentally impacts upon democratic debate in the public sphere and generates forms of false consciousness while concealing the vested interests that informs its communications.

'Opinion management' is distinguished from advertising by the fact that it expressly lays claim to the public sphere as one that plays a role in the political realm. Private advertisements are always directed to other private people insofar as they are consumers; the addressee of public relations is 'public opinion', or the private citizens as the public and not directly as consumers. The sender of the message hides his business intentions in the role of someone interested in the public welfare.... Advertising limited itself by and large to the simple sales pitch. In contrast, opinion management with its 'promotion' and 'exploitation' goes beyond advertising; it invades the process of 'public opinion' by systematically creating news events or exploiting events that attract attention.... Public relations fuses both: advertisement must absolutely not be recognizable as the self-presentation of a private interest. It bestows on its object the authority of an object of public interest about which – this is the illusion to be created – the public of critically reflecting private people freely forms its opinion.

Habermas (1991: 193–194)

Habermas' perspective has informed many subsequent social science, communications and media and cultural studies accounts. Miller and Dinan (2008) argue that PR acts as the tool of political and corporate elites that has been used to diminish democratic processes. In effect, PR has been 'a means for "taking the risk" out of democracy' for powerful corporations, ensuring their dominance (Miller and Dinan 2007: 11). Heller (2016: 662) notes the historically embedded character of PR's relationship to corporate power: 'PR was developed in the interwar period as a discourse to harness the rise of mass media, to promote and justify the corporation, and to protect them from public criticism. It developed both defensive and positive functions through its role in media relations and the creation of corporate identity'. Bourdieu (2000) sees PR practitioners as cultural intermediaries who engage in subtle but insidious forms of influence. They can manipulate symbolic capital in ways which can legitimise and extend certain power relations (Edwards 2008, 2012; Ihlen 2009). PR has been seen as a key player in a new form of 'commercial democracy' which forges a novel relationship between political culture and commercial culture (Cronin 2018). Others have seen PR as a form of stealth communication (Curry

Jansen 2017) which can both manipulate and conceal: 'Those who examine the role of international PR under neoliberalism will find that there are many toxic secrets to be excavated and subjected to critical illumination' (Curry Jansen 2016: 14).

In much of the critical literature on PR, there has been an emphasis on power and how PR can shape power relations. In politics, PR's work in lobbying, media management and in generating 'spin' has been the focus of some interesting critical attention (e.g. Cave & Rowell 2014; Davis 2002; Ewen 1996; Fisher 2017; Garland 2017; McNair 2004). More generally, PR has been understood as a form of propaganda, as in Wimberly's (2020) historical account of the development of PR in the United States:

> Propaganda is not different from public relations except in its name: public relations and propaganda name the same activities, the same rationalization of those activities, and even the same personages. They are the same except that public relations is a kind of doubling of propaganda, in that the term 'public relations' is propaganda for propaganda.
>
> Wimberley (2020: 2)

In this view, PR manages public opinion and attempts conceal the processes of management that it deploys. Similarly, Moloney and McGrath (2020: 6) argue that PR is a form of 'weak propaganda' as it involves producing and shaping communication that, 'encourages the receiver to act in a particular way: to accept the group or organisational perspective, to write a news story for their paper, to drive more carefully, to support a policy or politician, to be a more motivated and productive employee'.[6] This critical strand can also be identified in accounts of the PR industry by practitioners themselves. Robert Phillips, for instance, characterises the industry as, 'the ugly child of bad politics, bad market economics and the misguided corporatism that enshrined them' (2015: 134).

But there are also a significant number of analyses, often emerging from the disciplinary field of public relations, which argue that public relations can be a force for good. It is argued, for instance, that PR has the potential to facilitate genuine public engagement between organisations, governments and publics and can act in the public interest (e.g. Brunner & Smallwood 2019; Hodges & McGrath 2011; Johnston 2016, 2017; Johnston & Pieczka 2018; Munshi & Kurian 2020), and that PR can be used by some of the least powerful groups in society to further goals of social justice (Demetrious 2013).

The context of UK PR and media today

There have been significant changes in the UK PR industry and the media context in which it operates which impact on PR practitioners' everyday work and which shape the contexts in which practices of secrecy are situated. I discuss some of the key changes below with reference to the interview material from my study.

The promotional field in the United Kingdom is shifting such that the relationship between, and relative financial strength, of the various elements of advertising, marketing and PR has altered. The respondents in my study noted how clients have shifted their promotional budget away from advertising, a trend which has been ongoing for some time now (see Ofcom 2021). As Francis Ingham, Director General of the trade body the PRCA, describes, 'there's been the blending of disciplines, so the dividing line between advertising and PR, marketing is... incredibly blurred now. There's been a shift in spend, that's been quite pronounced, away from advertising towards PR.... It's value for money.... People used to say they had an advertising budget and they had a PR budget, now they have a, how do you frame it? Reputation budget, I suppose'. Many of the respondents in my study noted how the media landscape has fragmented and how the remit of media relations PR now extends beyond writing press releases and liaising with journalists. Phil Morgan of the CIPR describes this shift: 'it's meant that media relations is no longer just about newspapers, about dealing with journalists. It's meant that media relations is now about managing media literally as channels.... It's very different to writing for media releases, writing for newspapers... or generally doing sort of the very functional, traditional media relations stuff.... Now it's very much more instantaneous but it's also a two-way channel'. Within the industry, there is a general sense that communications should be a form of engagement or dialogue with PR's audiences or readers, and this view is well represented in the literature on PR (for example, see Edwards 2018; Johnston 2016). One PR practitioner in my study describes this transformation: '[in the past] it was very much about central communications pushing out press releases and stories... you are part of a conversation now. It's very much [that] you have to listen to the world and what people are saying' (participant 12). There are, of course, questions to be asked about the extent to which such dialogue or engagement is genuinely motivated and has positive impact (Cronin 2018; Curry Jansen 2016; Miller & Dinan 2008, 2007; Ihlen & Levenshus 2017; Moloney & McGrath 2020), but the principle of dialogue and two-way engagement has now become a core part of the PR industry's sense of its own mission and the way PR agencies present themselves publicly.

Media relations PR practice focuses increasingly on social media as the route to engage publics in dialogue and to further their clients' interests (Thurlow 2019; see Shoai 2021 for a discussion of the promise of social media for the PR industry). PR has developed new techniques through the affordances offered by digital technologies – as I discuss in Chapter 3 – and it has been noted that PR's engagement with social media in particular can intersect in powerful ways with broader social phenomena such as that of 'post-truth' and cultures of disinformation (Thompson 2020). In fact, the PR industry can turn issues of disinformation to its advantage by framing its communication expertise as the answer to the high profile problem of 'fake news', thus enhancing the industry's professional legitimacy and diverting attention from its own questionable practices (Edwards 2021).

Despite the changes in the media sphere and their impact on everyday PR practices, PR respondents in my study consistently stated that the core aims and tasks of media relations PR remain unchanged, although there is often much industry discussion about novelty and innovation: 'actually, what underpins [PR work] which is things like understanding your audiences, clarifying messaging, understanding reputational risk and how to mitigate that. Those things – thinking about brand, thinking about tone of voice, none of those things have changed' (participant 11). Like other promotional industries such as advertising (see Cronin 2004), PR can fetishise innovation and inflate the value of what is perceived as new, as one very experienced PR practitioner noted:

> PR is an industry which frustratingly does not build on the past. It believes that human behaviour is renewed constantly and therefore… if you're not at the very leading edge of how tech is used to communicate with people then you know you can't possibly understand what people's motivations are and that is demonstrably wrong. And the evidence for that is that when I began my career 35 years ago, people believed exactly the same as they do now. So, in 35 years the industry hasn't changed in the way that it fetishizes the new, shiny thing. But the irony is that that is exactly unchanged over time… its obsession with change is unchanging.
>
> Nigel Sarbutts (participant 29)

The respondents in my study also commented that despite developments in technology and changes in the media sphere, there is considerable continuity in what clients want from PR: 'your tools and channels are changing [but] I think what companies want from PR hasn't changed. I think [clients] still want PR there to help them get their messages out, help them make money, help them hide messages that they don't want getting out' (participant 28). In Chapter 3, I discuss the means by which PR practitioners help clients conceal, or divert attention from, troubling issues. This captures a core concern of PR practice: the promotion of clients' interests, usually centred on profit, influence or, in the case of charities, the enhancement of brand and fundraising potential (see Ihlen & Levenshus 2017). PR is sometimes discussed within the industry as the 'conscience' or the 'ethical guardian' of an organisation which is tasked to uphold values (Jackson & Moloney 2019; L'Etang 2003). But, as one PR practitioner in my study noted, PR's core function is to support a client's financial bottom-line which may involve practices in tension with 'conscience' or 'ethics':

> Some people see PR as almost a conscience of the organisation and the conscience would be saying, 'actually, no, we shouldn't do that, you know, we've got to be ethical'. I think... in an ideal world [PR] wants to position itself as the one that says, 'let's not do that'.... It's hard, though, because... if you look at the [PR] textbooks [they] say we're all about supporting the business and the bottom-line. So that's really hard because actually if it's through unethical practices that you drive profits, then where does PR put itself?
>
> (participant 28)

As noted above, a significant proportion of PR work relies on the media in various ways, and on journalism in particular. As I discuss in more detail in Chapter 4, journalism has long been seen as a crucial mechanism for circulating information and creating a space for democratic debate (Gans 2003; Habermas 1991; Schudson 2018). But journalism is today under intense pressure and the media finance models that support journalism are under severe strain. The Cairncross Review, which was tasked to examine the state of UK journalism, reports on this ongoing financial trend: 'Revenues from advertising and sales of printed newspapers dropped by 50% between 2007 and 2017. For most publishers, online advertising revenue has not come close to compensating for the decline in print revenue' (Cairncross 2019: 39).[7] This massive shift in media finance models has had far-reaching consequences, including a notable reduction in the number of journalists: 'As a result of falling revenues, publishers have cut costs dramatically. This has hurt the provision of all types of public-interest news, but local level democracy reporting the most' (Cairncross 2019: 9). The Review also noted that despite falling sales and a contraction in staffing, newspapers and 'written journalism' still has a significant impact on the field, particularly through their interface with broadcast journalism:

> Although news can be found on television and radio, written journalism (whether in print or online) supplies the largest quantity of original journalism and is most at risk.… Newspapers, in other words, still play the central role in financing the creation of original journalism, accounting for as much as broadcasting and online put together. Thus, broadcasters are more likely to carry news stories that have first appeared in newspapers, rather than vice versa.
>
> Cairncross (2019: 7, 18)

The changes in the field of journalism have significant and wide-reaching implications. But rather than provide such an overview of news culture, I restrict my focus to the relationship between public relations and the news media, and the ways they mediate secrecy and publicity.

Alongside the new opportunities offered by social media platforms, PR practitioners now have increased chances of securing media coverage in 'traditional' or 'legacy' media such as newspapers and television news media outlets. Journalists' workloads have intensified as journalist numbers have diminished and far more news content is required for the range of online media sites and social media feeds (Cairncross 2019). The decline in the number of journalists can be contrasted with the increase in the size and revenue of the PR industry – globally, the PR industry is projected to grow from $92.55 billion in 2021 to $102.80 billion in 2022.[8] PR can also circumvent journalists as the traditional route to securing media coverage by using the 'owned media' of their clients (web sites and social media). The journalists, editors and PR practitioners in my study were well aware of this trend and how it impacts on the everyday practices in both journalism and PR. As John Harrington, the editor of the trade newspaper *PR Week*, described to me,

> I think the biggest change has been the relative decline in the number of journalists on news desks and so on, and then the relevant increase in the number of PRs, so I think there's probably less time for journalists to work on stories, which can mean there's an opportunity for PRs to have perhaps more sway if they're putting

things together in a way that the journalists want them. And on the other hand, there's quite a lot of PRs that know you don't necessarily need to always go through journalists now... the rise of influencer marketing, for example, has had an impact, the rise of... [a] brand's own channels, and you look at some organisations that specifically exclude journalists, so, for example, the Boris Johnson campaign excluding the *Mirror* [newspaper] from their election buff. I don't think that would have happened in the last election.

I discuss the significance of these developments for PR in more detail in later chapters, but here it is sufficient to note that the pressure that journalists and news sites face offers PR practitioners an enhanced opportunity to secure media coverage for clients as journalists may rely increasingly on material provided in PR press releases in what Gandy (1982) famously called 'information subsidies' (see Cronin 2018; Forde & Johnston 2013; Jackson & Moloney 2016; Lewis et al. 2008; McChesney 2012; Phillips 2010). As Francis Ingham, Director General of the trade body the PRCA, reported to me, '[some of] my members would see the slow decline of journalism... as an opportunity, honestly... because if you can give journalists content that they're eager to use, then that's easier to convey your message'. As well as shaping the content of news reporting, this reliance on PR press releases contributes to a growing homogeneity of content across the media sphere. In their analysis of online news, Redden and Witschge (2010) found that this homogeneity derived from the reliance on press releases and material from wire services or press agencies such as Reuters, and on the recycling of material from their own news sites. Jim Waterson, Media Editor of *The Guardian* newspaper, summarises the growing influence of PR,

> Journalism as a whole is painfully reliant on PR. At the lower end of the market it props it up enormously in terms of consumer PR and feeding out stories on product launches and things like that. At the mid-market, it's also increasingly adopting that approach, and at the high end even there it's nibbling round the edges in terms of controlling access to people that you would want to interview.

PR's control of access to sources was noted by one of the journalists in my study. As a highly experienced journalist who has worked for a range of national newspapers described, he now struggles to gain direct access to sources, even those with whom he has a good relationship: '[even] in a relatively innocent situation, PRs intrude themselves... in order to ensure that [their bosses are] not going to face any difficult questions' (Roy Greenslade).

Analysing secrecy and publicity in the news media sphere

In order to analyse the play of secrecy and publicity in PR and its interface with the news media, I will draw on Michel Foucault's work. As the discussion in previous sections demonstrates, secrecy and publicity practices are materially embedded – in legislation, in social norms, in the material affordances of technologies, in the social practices of individuals and groups, in power relations, in media finance models and so on. At the same time, they circulate in more diffuse forms through ideas, images, narratives, rumour, gossip and conspiracy theories. Foucault famously described the shift in forms of power in European societies linked to transformations in regimes of visibility. His account of the development of disciplinary power was centred on the rendering transparent of what had previously been obscure, describing Bentham's panopticon as a 'project of a universal visibility which exists to serve a rigorous, meticulous power' (1980: 152). This was a transparency project which generated new ways of understanding individuals and societies and created new formations of power.

> A fear haunted the latter half of the eighteenth century: the fear of darkened spaces, of the pall of gloom which prevents the full visibility of things, men and truths. It sought to break up the patches of darkness that blocked the light, eliminate the shadowy areas of society, demolish the unlit chambers where arbitrary political acts, monarchical caprice, religious superstitions, tyrannical and priestly plots, epidemics and the illusions of ignorance were fomented... If Bentham's project aroused interest, this was because it provided a formula applicable to many domains, the formula of 'power through transparency', subjection by 'illumination'.
> Foucault (1980: 153–154)

Disciplinary and bio-power – the new power over life itself – developed through visibility, monitoring and self-monitoring, leaving only death as the secret zone that escapes the gaze of power: 'Now it is over life, throughout its unfolding, that power establishes its domination; death is power's limit, the moment that escapes it; death becomes the most secret aspect of existence, the most "private"' (Foucault 1990: 138). Foucault's work can also help analyse the urge for revelation that is stitched into secrecy practices. In his account of the 'will to knowledge', Foucault argues that we need to appreciate the appeal of seeking and revealing truth: 'the pleasure of knowing that truth, of discovering and exposing it, the fascination of seeing it and telling it, of captivating and capturing others by it, of confiding it in secret, of luring it out in the open' (Foucault 1990: 71).

In later chapters, I develop Foucault's account of power and visibility in relation to secrecy and publicity in the media sphere. But here, I want to signal another conceptual framing that orients my argument: throughout the book, I develop Simmel's (1906) point that secrecy creates a 'second world' alongside the world that is visibly evident. Reframing this as the 'shadow world of the media sphere', I examine how PR and certain practices of journalism operate at the fulcrum of secrecy–publicity. It is not simply that PR enables secrecy through practices of concealment, and that journalism enables publicity, visibility or transparency through uncovering and circulating information. Both PR and journalism operate within complex dynamics of secrecy and publicity that emerge from, and in turn help shape, the media sphere. Jodi Dean (2002) dismisses Simmel's idea of a second world of secrecy as a fantasy offered to the public:

> This mystical possibility of a hidden world, this capacity to produce a realm beyond the given in which anything might happen, gives the secret an irresistible aura. What makes the exception produced by secrecy so attractive is the possibility of a hidden power, a power that can make new worlds as well as shape the old one.
>
> Dean (2002: 10)

In effect, Dean is suggesting that Simmel's 'second world' is part of, or can fuel, conspiracy theories that centre on imagining that everything is connected, that there are elite groups orchestrating the world and that the information is there to be uncovered with the right skills. However, we can acknowledge that there is a hidden realm, pockets of secrecy or a shadow world, without subscribing to conspiracy theory, or without succumbing to the seductions of 'secrecy thinking' (that is, being seduced into a never-ending search for concealed truths which are purportedly 'out there'). We can recognise that there are organised groups, nation-states and corporations which do, in fact, exert considerable power through their attempts to obscure information, interests and power dynamics. Consider the case of Facebook and its parent company Meta (see Neiborg & Helmond 2019) and the renewed academic interest in analysing propaganda, including state propaganda (e.g. Baines et al. 2020). In PR, news media and the media sphere, more broadly, we can see a range of material practices which interface with the law, codes of practice and financial and corporate exigencies that create zones of unintelligibility or pockets of secrecy which have a tangible impact on societies and potentially on their democratic practices. Such pockets of secrecy are enabled by the specific patterning of media practice and I examine their operation in detail in the following chapters using empirical data from interviews and a discussion of examples. The next chapter focuses on the range of techniques that media relations PR uses in order to manipulate the secrecy–publicity dynamic for the benefit of its clients.

Notes

1 In a somewhat similar vein, Boltanski (1994) explores how the instability of the nation-state, the contested nature of reality, and the role of conspiracy are dramatised in crime and spy novels.
2 Goffman (1959) also discussed secrets, concealment and fabrication in relation to his framework of backstage behaviour.
3 See Harrington (2021) on secrecy and wealth.
4 Dean also argues that we are interpellated as celebrities: 'a drive to be known, and the presumption that what matters is what is known, provides a different economy of subjectivization, one in which the technocultural subject is configured as a celebrity' (2002: 12–13).
5 Despite the range of critiques directed at PR from academic studies, the general public, the media, and some politicians, the industry is largely unregulated, although some sectors such as financial PR are bound by certain regulatory frameworks (see Bourne 2017).
6 Discussion of PR's potential status as propaganda is ongoing (see for example Holbrook 2014; Lock and Ludolph 2020).
7 It is interesting to note that although the Cairncross Review (2019) explored both the negative impact of fake news on a healthy democratic news sphere and the growing role of algorithms in shaping the news that is presented to the public in online settings, it did not examine the issue of news media's reliance on press releases and other PR material for content.
8 https://www.thebusinessresearchcompany.com/report/public-relations-global-market-report. Accessed 19/4/22.

References

Arendt, H. (1951) *The Burden of Our Time*. London: Secker & Warburg.
Bail, C. A. (2015) 'The public life of secrets: deception, disclosure, and discursive framing in the policy process', *Sociological Theory*, 33(2): 97–124.
Baines, P., N. O'Shaughnessy, & N. Snow (eds) (2020) *The Sage Handbook of Propaganda*. London: Sage.

Barnwell, A. (2019) 'Family secrets and the slow violence of social stigma', *Sociology*, 53(6): 1111–1126.

Birchall, C. (2021) *Radical Secrecy: The Ends of Transparency in Datafied America*. Minneapolis, MN: University of Minnesota Press.

Birchall, C. (2016) 'Managing secrecy', *International Journal of Communication*, 10: 152–163.

Birchall, C. (2014) 'Radical transparency?', *Cultural Studies ↔ Critical Methodologies*, 14(1): 77–88.

Bok, S. (1989) *Secrets: On the Ethics of Concealment and Revelation*. New York: Vintage Books.

Boltanski, L. (1994) *Mysteries and Conspiracies: Detective Stories, Spy Novels and the Making of Modern Societies*, trans. Catherine Porter. Cambridge, MA: Polity.

Bourdieu, P. (2000) *Distinction: A Social Critique of the Judgement of Taste*. London: Routledge.

Bourne, C. (2017) *Trust, Power and Public Relations in Financial Markets*. London & New York: Routledge.

Boyle, K. (2019) *#MeToo, Weinstein and Feminism*. Cham: Palgrave.

Brighenti, A. (2007) 'Visibility: A category for the social sciences', *Current Sociology* 55(3): 323–342.

Brunner, B. R. & A. M. K. Smallwood (2019) 'Prioritizing public interest in public relations: public interest relations', *Public Relations Inquiry*, 8(3): 245–264.

Cairncross, F. (2019) *The Cairncross Review: A Sustainable Future for Journalism*. https://assets.publishing.service.gov.uk/government/uploads/system/uploads/attachment_data/file/779882/021919_DCMS_Cairncross_Review_.pdf. Accessed 19/4/22.

Cave, T. & A. Rowell (2014) *A Quiet Word: Lobbying, Crony Capitalism and Broken Politics in Britain*. London: The Bodley Head.

CIPR (2020) *State of the Profession 2020*. Downloaded from: https://www.cipr.co.uk/CIPR/Our_work/Policy/CIPR_State_of_the_Profession_2019_20.aspx. Accessed 3/3/22.

Costas, J & C. Grey (2016) *Secrecy at Work: The Hidden Architecture of Organizational Life*. Stanford, CA: Stanford University Press.

Cronin, A. M. (2018) *Public Relations Capitalism: Promotional Culture, Publics and Commercial Democracy*. Basingstoke: Palgrave Macmillan.

Cronin, A. M. (2004) *Advertising Myths: The Strange Half-Lives of Images and Commodities*. London & New York: Routledge.

Curry Jansen, S. (2017) *Stealth Communication: The Spectacular Rise of Public Relations*. Cambridge & Malden, MA: Polity.

Curry Jansen, S. (2016) 'Secrecy, confidentiality and "dirty work": the case of public relations', *Secrecy and Society*, 1(1): 1–16.

Davies, N. (2009) *Flat Earth News: An Award-winning Reporter Exposes Falsehood, Distortion and Propaganda in the Global Media*. London: Vintage.

Davis, A. (2002) *Public Relations Democracy: Public Relations, Politics and the Mass Media in Britain*. Manchester: Manchester University Press.

Dean, J. (2019) 'Communicative capitalism and revolutionary form', *Millennium: Journal of International Studies*, 47(3): 326–340.

Dean, J. (2009) *Democracy and Other Neoliberal Fantasies: Communicative Capitalism and Left Politics*. Durham, NC: Duke University Press.

Dean, J. (2005) 'Communicative capitalism: circulation and the foreclosure of politics', *Cultural Politics*, 1(1): 51–74.

Dean, J. (2002) *Publicity's Secret: How Technoculture Capitalizes on Democracy*. New York: Cornell University Press.

Debord, G. (1998) *Comments on the Society of the Spectacle*, trans. Imrie M. London & New York: Verso.

Debord, G. (1995) *The Society of the Spectacle*, trans. Donald Nicholson Smith. New York: Zone Books.

Demetrious, K. (2019) "Energy wars': global PR and public debate in the 21st century', *Public Relations Inquiry*, 8(1): 7–22.

Demetrious, K. (2013) *Public Relations, Activism, and Social Change*. London & New York: Routledge.

Derrida, J. (1994) '"To Do Justice to Freud": the history of madness in the age of psychoanalysis', *Critical Inquiry*, 20(2): 227–266.

Edwards, L. (2021) 'Organised lying and professional legitimacy: public relations' accountability in the disinformation debate', *European Journal of Communication*, 36(2): 168–182.

Edwards, L. (2018) *Understanding Public Relations: Theory, Culture and Society*. London: Sage.

Edwards, L. (2012) 'Exploring the role of public relations as a cultural intermediary occupation', *Cultural Sociology*, 6(4): 438–454.

Edwards, L. (2008) 'PR practitioners' cultural capital: an initial study and implications for research and practice', *Public Relations Review*, 34: 367–372.

Etzioni, A. (2010) 'Is transparency the best disinfectant?', *The Journal of Political Philosophy* 18(4): 389–404.

Ewen, S. (1996) *PR! A Social History of Spin*. New York: Basic Books.

Featherstone, M. (1991) 'Georg Simmel: an introduction', *Theory, Culture and Society*, 8(3): 1–16.

Flyverbom, M. (2016) 'Transparency: mediation and the management of visibilities', *International Journal of Communication*, 10: 110–122.

Fenster, M. (2014) 'The implausibility of secrecy', *Hastings Law Journal*, 65(2): 309–363.

Fisher, C. (2017) 'Re-assessing the "Public's Right to Know": the shift from journalism to political PR', *Journalism Studies*, 18(3): 358–375.

Forde, S. & J. Johnston (2013) 'The news triumvirate: public relations, wire agencies and online copy', *Journalism Studies*, 14(1): 113–129.

Foucault, M. (2007) *Security, Territory, Population: Lectures at the College de France, 1977–78*. A. I. Davidson (ed). Basingstoke: Palgrave Macmillan.

Foucault, M. (1990) *The History of Sexuality, Volume 1*, trans. Robert Hurley. London: Penguin.

Foucault, M. (1980) *Power/Knowledge: Selected Interviews and Other Writings, 1972–1977*. C. Gordon (ed). New York: Pantheon Books.

Frisby, D. (1992) *Simmel and Since: Essays on Georg Simmel's Social Theory.* London & New York: Routledge.

Frisby, D. (1986) *Fragments of Modernity: Theories of Modernity in the Work of Simmel, Kracauer and Benjamin.* Cambridge: The MIT Press.

Gandy, O. H. (1982) *Beyond Agenda Setting: Information Subsidies and Public Policy.* New York: Ablex.

Gans, H. J. (2003) *Democracy and the News.* Oxford: Oxford University Press.

Garland, R. (2017) 'Between mediatisation and politicisation: The changing role and position of Whitehall press officers in the age of political spin', *Public Relations Inquiry*, 6(2): 171–189.

Gibson-Graham, J. K. (2006) *A Postcapitalist Politics.* London & Minneapolis: University of Minnesota Press.

Gibson-Graham, J. K. (1996) *The End of Capitalism (As We Knew It): A Feminist Critique of Political Economy.* Cambridge, MA & Oxford: Blackwell.

Gilbert, J. (2007) 'Public secrets: "Being-with" in an era of perpetual disclosure', *Cultural Studies*, 21(1): 22–41.

Goffman, E. (1959) *Presentation of Self in Everyday Life.* New York: Doubleday.

Habermas, J. (1991) *The Structural Transformation of the Public Sphere.* Cambridge: MIT Press.

Harrington, B. (2021) 'Secrecy, Simmel and the new sociology of wealth', *Sociologica*, 15(2). https://doi.org/10.6092/issn.1971-8853/13565

Heller, M. (2016) 'Foucault, discourse, and the birth of British public relations', *Enterprise & Society*, 17(3): 651–677.

Herdt, G. (1990) 'Secret societies and secret collectives', *Oceania*, 60(4): 360–381.

Hodges, C. E.M. and N. McGrath (2011) 'Communication for social transformation', in L. Edwards and C. E.M Hodges (eds) *Public Relations, Society and Culture.* London & New York: Routledge. pp. 90–104.

Holbrook, D. (2014) 'Approaching terrorist public relations initiatives', *Public Relations Inquiry*, 3(2): 141–161.

Horn, E. (2013) *The Secret War: Treason, Espionage, and Modern Fiction*, trans. Geoffrey Winthrop-Young. Evanston, IL: Northwestern University Press.

Horn. E. (2011) 'Logics of political secrecy', *Theory, Culture & Society*, 28(7–8): 103–122.

Ihlen, Ø. (2009) 'On Bourdieu: public relations in field struggles', in O. Ihlen, B van Ruler, M. Fredriksson (eds) *Public Relations and Social Theory.* New York: Routledge. pp. 62–82.

Ihlen, Ø. & A. Levenshus (2017) 'Panacea, placebo or prudence: perspectives and constraints for corporate dialogue', *Public Relations Inquiry*, 6(3): 219–232.

Jackson, D. & K. Moloney (2019) '"Uneasy lies the head that wears a crown": a qualitative study of ethical PR practice in the United Kingdom', *Public Relations Inquiry*, 8(1): 87–101.

Jackson, D. & K. Moloney (2016) 'Inside churnalism: PR, journalism and power relationships in flux', *Journalism Studies*, 17(6): 763–780.

Johnston, J. (2017) 'The public interest: a new way of thinking for public relations?', *Public Relations Inquiry*, 6(1): 5–22.

Johnston, J. (2016) *Public Relations and the Public Interest*. New York & London: Routledge.

Johnston J. and M. Pieczka (eds) (2018) *Public Interest Communication: Critical Debates and Global Contexts*. London: Routledge.

Jones, G.M. (2014) 'Secrecy', *Annual Review of Anthropology*, 43: 53–69.

Lefebvre, S. (2021) 'The rhetorical devices of the keepers of state secrets', *Secrecy and Society*, 2(2): https://doi.org/10.31979/2377-6188.2021.020206

L'Etang, J. (2003) 'The myth of the "ethical guardian": an examination of its origins, potency and illusions', *Journal of Communication Management*, 8(1): 53–67.

Lewis, J., A. Williams & B. Franklin (2008) 'A compromised fourth estate? UK journalism, public relations and news sources', *Journalism Studies*, 9(1): 1–20.

Lock, I. & R. Ludolph (2020) 'Organizational propaganda on the Internet: a systematic review', *Public Relations Inquiry*, 9(1): 103–127.

Lukács, G. (1991) 'Georg Simmel', *Theory, Culture and Society*, 8(3): 145–150.

Nieborg, D. B. and A. Helmond (2019) 'The political economy of Facebook's platformization in the mobile ecosystem: Facebook Messenger as a platform instance', *Media, Culture & Society*, 41(2): 196–218.

McChesney, R. W. (2012) 'Farewell to journalism?', *Journalism Studies*, 13(5–6): 682–694.

McNair, B. (2004) 'PR must die: spin, anti-spin and political public relations in the UK 1997–2004', *Journalism Studies*, 5(3): 325–338.

Marx, K. (1990) *Capital: A Critique of Political Economy*, Volume 1, trans. Ben Fowles. London: Penguin.

Masco, J. (2010) '"Sensitive but unclassified": secrecy and the counterterrorist state', *Public Culture*, 22(3): 433–463.

Melley, T. (2012) *The Covert Sphere: Secrecy, Fiction, and the National Security State*, New York: Cornell University Press.

Miller, D. & W. Dinan (2008) *A Century of Spin: How Public Relations Became the Cutting Edge of Corporate Power*. London: Pluto Press.

Miller, D. & W. Dinan (2007) 'Public relations and the subversion of democracy', in D. W. Dinan & D. Miller (eds) *Thinker, Faker, Spinner, Spy: Corporate PR and the Assault on Democracy*. London: Pluto Press. pp. 11–20.

Moloney, K. & C. McGrath (2020) *Rethinking Public Relations: Persuasion, Democracy and Society* (3rd ed). London: Routledge.

Moore, S. (2018) 'Towards a sociology of institutional transparency: openness, deception and the problem of public trust', *Sociology*, 52(2): 416–430.

Mundt, M., K. Ross & C. M. Burnett (2018) 'Scaling social movements through social media: the case of black lives matter', *Social Media + Society*. https://doi.org/10.1177/2056305118807911

Munshi, D, & P. Kurian (2020) *Public Relations and Sustainable Citizenship: Representing the Unrepresented.* London & New York: Routledge.

OFCOM (2021) *Media Nations: UK 2021.* https://www.ofcom.org.uk/__data/assets/pdf_file/0023/222890/media-nations-report-2021.pdf. Accessed 14/4/22.

Phillips, A. (2010) 'Old sources: new bottles. Journalists and their sources online' in N. Fenton (ed) *New Media, Old News: Journalism and democracy in a Digital Age.* London: Sage. pp. 87–101.

Phillips, R. (2015) *Trust Me, PR is Dead.* London: Unbound.

Poell, T. (2014) 'Social media and the transformation of activist communication: exploring the social media ecology of the 2010 Toronto G20 protests', *Information, Communication & Society*, 17(6): 716–731.

PRCA (2020) *PR and Communications Census 2020.* Downloaded from https://news.prca.org.uk/empathy-and-ethics-must-form-the-heart-of-prs-recovery-2020-prca-pr-census/. Accessed 3/3/22.

Redden, J. & T. Witschge (2010) 'A new news order? Online news content examined', in N. Fenton (ed) *New Media, Old News: Journalism and democracy in a Digital Age.* London: Sage. pp. 171–186.

Schudson, M. (2020) 'The Shortcomings of Transparency for Democracy', *American Behavioral Scientist*, 64(11): 1670–1678.

Schudson, M. (2018) *Why Journalism Still Matters.* Cambridge, MA: Polity Press.

Shilling, C. & P. A. Mellor (2015) 'For a sociology of deceit: doubled identities, interested actions and situational logics of opportunity', *Sociology*, 49(4): 607–623.

Shoai, A. (2021) 'Dealing with disappointment: How can a "coexisting imperatives" view help us understand the unfulfilled dialogical promise of digital media', *Public Relations Inquiry.* https://doi.org/10.1177/2046147X211045630

Simmel, G. (2004) *The Philosophy of Money.* David Frisby (ed), trans. T. Bottomore & D. Frisby. London & New York: Routledge.

Simmel, G. (1906) 'The sociology of secrecy and of secret societies', *American Journal of Sociology*, 11(4): 441–498.

Smart, C. (2011) 'Families, secrets and memories', *Sociology*, 45(4): 539–553.

Taussig, M. (1999) *Defacement: Public Secrecy and the Labor of the Negative.* Stanford, CA: Stanford University Press.

Tench, R. & L. Yeomans (2009) *Exploring Public Relations.* Harlow: Prentice Hall.

Thompson, G. (2020) *Post-Truth Public Relations: Communication in an Era of Digital Disinformation.* London & New York: Routledge.

Thurlow, A. (2019) *Social Media, Organizational Identity and Public Relations: The Challenge of Authenticity.* London: Routledge.

Vincent, D. (1998) *The Culture of Secrecy: Britain 1832–1998.* Oxford: Oxford University Press.

Weber, M. (1997) *From Max Weber: Essays in Sociology.* Gerth H. H. & Wright Mills C (ed). London: Routledge.

Wimberly, C. (2020) *How Propaganda Became Public Relations: Foucault and the Corporate Government of the Public.* New York & London: Taylor & Francis.

Wright Mills, C. (1959) *The Power Elite.* New York: Oxford University Press.

Žižek, S. (1989) *The Sublime Object of Ideology.* London: Verso.

3 PR techniques of secrecy and publicity

This chapter draws on Georg Simmel's account of secrecy in order to analyse empirical material relating to PR's interface with both secrecy and 'publicity' (the making public of information or interests) (Simmel 1906: 469). Practices of secrecy, which exist in all societies in varying forms according to Simmel, actively create a 'second world' which is hidden from view but which exerts an influence on 'the obvious world', or that which is visible to the general public (Simmel 1906: 462). I argue that media relations PR and its practices of secrecy and publicity is one of many forces that acts to create a 'second world' or, in my terms, a shadow world of the media sphere. Drawing on empirical material including interviews and examples, this chapter outlines a range of PR practices and analyses their relationship to both 'publicity' and to secrecy, and explores how they intersect with the dynamics of the secrecy–publicity relationship. In a Foucaultian vein, I frame these practices as 'technologies of secrecy' and 'technologies of publicity' in order to highlight their impact as modes of governance.

As noted in the previous chapters, the field of PR practice comprises a wide range of specialisms and the techniques it uses to conceal, to manage information, to enhance reputation and to exert influence are equally diverse. For example, one branch of PR, known as Public Affairs, focuses its efforts on lobbying. A sector such as UK farming might, for instance, employ PR agencies or in-house PR practitioners through its trade body the National Farmers Union to lobby the UK government on matters such as proposed legislation that may affect that sector.[1] Practices such as lobbying are attempts to exert influence on behalf of PR's clients and, although not technically secret, many of these practices and the interests that direct them remain obscure – and it is in the interests of PR firms' clients that they remain so.[2] Rather than lobbying or Public Affairs, this study's focus is the sector of PR

DOI: 10.4324/9781003369585-3

called media relations as it most directly impacts upon the media sphere and the dynamics of the secrecy–publicity relationship. While many of the PR media management techniques that I will discuss are evidently secrecy-based practices, other techniques initially appear less oriented by secrecy. However, in this chapter and the next, I will demonstrate that a wide range of PR techniques draw on the *dynamic tension* that exists between secrecy and publicity (and publicity's dominant discursive manifestation today as 'transparency'), and in this way actively shape the impact of secrecy on society. Understanding PR practices through the lens of secrecy–publicity offers a productive entry point for better appreciating PR's complex social influence. PR is embedded in – and acts to reshape – social (not simply communicative) practices and the secrecy–publicity dynamic is an important vector for this influence.

PR media management practices: technologies of publicity and secrecy

Accentuating the positive

In order to downplay or outweigh negative media stories about a client, PR deploys as a core technique the production and dissemination of positive narratives and associations. This is well recognised in the literature on PR (e.g. Brunner 2019; Edwards 2018; L'Etang 2008; Moloney & McGrath 2020). PR practitioners themselves identify this strategy of accentuating the positive and minimising reputational damage to organisations as a pivotal element of their role. As one PR practitioner in my study commented, clients 'want to put the information out there that puts them in the best light' (participant 6). Another PR practitioner describes how press releases may be structured to highlight a positive element in an otherwise negative situation in the hope that journalists will select that as the more interesting angle to report:

> ...a company is releasing its interim report, for example, and profits are down by 30%... but within that 60 page interim report there's highlights... 'we've launched the new office in Yorkshire, we've acquired this company here, we've invested in a community relations exercise here', and then you know you'd obviously look to lead on the positive stuff as you release that interim report in the hope that reporters would just take it verbatim and the fact that profits are down, you know, is buried in a press release or not

focused on at all. If they've acquired this company and they've got an intention to acquire more, that can obviously be a more interesting story than profits are down by 30%.

(participant 8)

Organisations will often attempt to outweigh the impact of negative stories about them by engaging in various Corporate Social Responsibility (CSR) practices and charity projects alongside a vigorous communications strategy (see Visser et al. 2010). Such practices are widely deployed after a crisis or specific instance of reputational damage to a client. One PR practitioner noted that oil and gas companies will attempt to alter their industry's negative associations by accentuating the positive through various reputation management techniques. They 'might be investing in a conservation project by the site or something and it's [about] making sure that the media are aware' (participant 27). Another PR practitioner commented that Amazon is a good example of such a strategy as, 'they're definitely on a mission to change their whole reputation about being a crappy place to work and you can see that in their comms' (participant 37). In response to their poor public image as an employer, a reputation compounded by widely circulating critiques of working conditions in their 'fulfilment centres', Amazon's corporate web site is at pains to present the company as transparent and 'socially aware'. In a section titled 'Curious about what happens behind the scenes when you shop Amazon?', the public and journalists are offered in-person or virtual tours of a fulfilment centre.[3] Amazon also engages in various CSR practices, for example, partnering with a charity to donate toys to children at Christmas. An Amazon press release from December 2021, 'Donate a Toy with Amazon UK and Charity In Kind Direct Delivering Smiles to Families in Need this Christmas[4] was taken up and recirculated in press outlets such as 'Ethical Marketing' almost word for word.[5]

Such positive narratives may be disseminated through clients' 'owned media' such as their own web sites and social media feeds. PR practitioners will also attempt to circulate these narratives through 'earned media', such as coverage in the mainstream media (alongside conventional 'paid media' such as advertising and marketing). There is a trend in which PR practitioners may now bypass journalists to achieve media coverage and instead use social media influencers (see Archer 2019; Coco & Eckert 2020; Davies & Hobbs 2020), focus on their owned media or exclude certain news outlets, as John Harrington, editor of the trade paper *PR Week*, notes,

Some organisations... specifically exclude journalists... you see things like Liverpool Football Club not letting *The Sun* [newspaper]

into their press conferences… I think there's this sense that if you're an organisation that really doesn't like a particular title, you can exclude them and you probably think, 'well, we'll be fine', because you know that the power of your own channels and also the power of whatever you're doing means that you can have that luxury. So, I think that does suggest a little bit of a tilt away from the [mainstream] media in some sense, but I also think that can be exaggerated.

While this technique of accentuating the positive is widely understood as one of the core tasks of everyday PR work, it is less widely appreciated as a technique or technology of secrecy. As the secrecy–publicity nexus is founded on a dynamic tension, PR efforts to outweigh any potential negative stories with positive narratives acts to conceal or render obscure those negatives.

Accentuating the positive in an attempt to balance out negative coverage is also evident in the increasingly wide use of Search Engine Optimisation (SEO) practices. These aim to push the corporation, brand, individual, or organisation up the list of results when certain search terms are used and thus to increase the client web site's 'domain authority' score, or how well a web site will rank on a search engine (see Schultheiß & Lewandowski 2021). As one PR practitioner states, 'SEO – you can kind of boost positive stories, can't you, and knock other stories down [the list of search results]' (participant 18). In effect, SEO can be used by PR to 'bury the bad news on Google' (participant 5, PR practitioner) by frontloading alternative positive stories and links in search results. As one PR practitioner observed, 'the saying is that Google never forgets, but it does de-optimize' (participant 16).

This technique of accentuating the positive may well be viewed in the PR industry and wider society as a reasonable and ethical practice in the context of a social system based on capitalism, market relations and market competition in which image and reputation are important forms of capital. But, the practice has the related effect of concealing issues which may impact negatively on organisations' image and profits, or indeed that which may be damaging to society. For instance, the SEO and PR practices of fossil fuel companies attempt a 'de-optimisation' of information circulating about the detrimental impact of their industry and products. Such companies also pay for positively inflected Google ads to appear next to search terms relating to energy, fossil fuels and climate change (McIntyre 2022), practices which have been called 'greenwashing' (see Munshi & Kurian 2020).

Distraction and diversion

Two related PR techniques or technologies of secrecy–publicity are
the practice of distracting public attention away from negative issues
relating to the client, and the diversion of journalistic attention from
issues that have the potential to become damaging stories. The deflection of the public gaze can be accomplished by using what has come
to be known as 'dead cats' – eye-catching stories released in the media
as distractions. One PR practitioner described the practice as part of
a repertoire of, 'easy tactical stuff, like bouncing dead cats around
the place which, you know, goes on every day' (participant 16). A former *Guardian* newspaper journalist, Gary Younge, describes how PR
practitioners might capitalise on the public appetite for entertaining
short items that circulate quickly and easily in both mainstream and
social media: 'so you would put out something funny and quick and
giff-like and silly, you know, and those always get distributed [in the
media] far quicker than anything that's serious or penetrating' (participant 22). A striking example is the claim that Boris Johnson made
in a TalkRadio interview in June 2019, the point at which he was vying
to become the UK's Prime Minister. When asked by a journalist what
he did to relax, he claimed that he made model buses out of wooden
wine boxes, painting in the bus passengers on the sides of the crates.
Unsurprisingly, this was reported widely in the media.[6] As well as
achieving publicity for (what he may have hoped came across as) his
irreverent, quirky and appealing character, Johnson's 'dead cat' also
functioned as a distraction and concealment tool. The amused media reporting of his claims, which then circulated even more widely
on social media, diverted public attention from the less-than-positive
aspects of his track record as London Mayor and specifically his association with the discredited claims on the side of the Vote Leave
campaign's 'Brexit bus' which promised that the NHS would receive
£350 million a week if Britain left the European Union. This 'dead cat'
also achieved a de-optimising effect on internet search engine results,
as searches for 'bus' and 'Johnson' would more likely find the model
bus claims rather than the discredited claims about £350 million for
the NHS.

PR distraction techniques can involve strategically releasing negative information about a client – which PR practitioners know will
eventually emerge but which needs to be managed – at the point when
it is hoped that the information will be subsumed by other dominant
stories circulating in the media. PR practitioners 'can time announce-
ments so they know they'll get buried. I mean there's a notorious

quote... from one of Tony Blair's former PR people that after 9/11 was a good day to bury bad news' (John Harrington, *PR Week* editor, participant 19). Combined with the speed of the news cycle, the information may never connect with the public and, if it does, the public may quickly disregard or forget it: 'sometimes the news agenda can move so quicky that... they can decide to release something on a certain day but then there will be other things going on and then the agenda moves too quickly, people will forget about things' (participant 19).

Another technique of distraction is the practice of camouflaging the damaging information in jargon in the hope that neither journalists nor the public will fully digest its significance. When discussing how PR practitioners could deflect attention away from an issue, John Harrington, *PR Week* editor, observed that, 'they could probably just spin it if they wanted to, and they could just massage figures or leave out certain parts of the information or bury the real story in jargon. And hope that with... depleted news desks no one will pick up on it'. PR can also attempt to divert journalistic attention away from potentially damaging stories by offering journalists an alternative story, or exclusive access to an interview, in return for not publishing the particular (negative) story that they had been pursuing. One PR practitioner describes this technique 'of giving something away, that you're happy to give away.... So giving little titbits of information that people might want without giving those main bits of information that might not necessarily paint the client, the organisation, an individual, in the best light' (participant 6). But as another PR practitioner notes, it is 'quite a short-term strategy because...the bad thing... will come out eventually. It can be filed away [by the journalist] for another time when you haven't got something in your bag that can distract' (participant 29). This dynamic relationship between concealment and revelation will be discussed in more detail in Chapter 4.

Another form of deflection or diversion is the defensive attack. For instance, a UK news story circulated in 2016 in which the then Labour Party leader Jeremy Corbyn was photographed sitting on the floor of a Virgin train after saying that he was unable to find a seat on a very busy journey.[7] Virgin trains took the very unusual step of releasing CCTV footage which they claimed showed available train seats, although this was disputed by various eyewitnesses. A standard PR response from a corporation would be to acknowledge the issue, provide context, apologise and indicate how they would make improvements to their service. However, Virgin's owner, Sir Richard Branson, took an alternative and very assertive stance, tweeting to challenge Corbyn's claims. Gary Younge, a former *Guardian* journalist, describes the scenario and the technique of defensive attack:

> Corbyn couldn't get a seat on a train... everybody's experienced that, I didn't understand why that was so controversial. That's a common experience and so then Virgin deflected that with a series of interventions that were kind of dishonest, or irrelevant... attacking Corbyn or attacking Labour... for which there was a market.... These things only work if there's a market for them, for the idea, for the disparagement or for the rescue. So you just kind of create another market, or you tap into another market.
>
> (participant 22)

The issue of privatised train travel, alongside over-crowded trains and high costs of travel, is a politically sensitive issue in the United Kingdom. Virgin's attack on Corbyn's claims merely drew critical media attention to the issue and to the Virgin brand, and gave Corbyn a media platform on which to present the Labour Party's perspective on the issue: 'Passengers across Britain will have been in similar situations on overcrowded, expensive trains. That is why our policy to bring the trains back into public ownership, as part of a plan to rebuild and transform Britain, is so popular with passengers and rail workers'.[8] In this instance, the defensive attack did not succeed and PR practitioners would advise against such a strategy in most cases.

'Data bombing' or 'snowing'

Important or damaging information can also be concealed by being hidden in plain sight in a mass release of insignificant information. Known as 'data bombing' or 'snowing' (and sometimes 'flooding'), this technique of secrecy has the advantage of appearing to be aligned with principles of transparency: it offers up data for scrutiny, but in practical terms makes it very difficult for journalists, other researchers or the general public to find and assess key information amid the plethora of data. In such cases, high levels of visibility of data, in fact, decrease genuine transparency (Stohl et al. 2016). In effect, important or damaging information can be concealed in complexity. But, PR narrative management techniques can also conceal issues, or foreclose nuanced understanding, in simplicity. One PR practitioner gave the example of Brexit slogans such as 'Take Back Control' or the UK government's Covid-19 advice to 'Stay Alert' as examples of communications techniques that 'reduce something right down to a slogan, it's so hard to debate it... you can just simplify it so much that you almost can't unpick it' (participant 28).

Difficulties relating to the volume of data and its interpretation also affect journalists' practices, and this issue is further compounded by reduced staffing levels. UK journalists' workloads have increased enormously as there are now fewer journalists and they face increased demands, such as the requirement to create online and social media content alongside their core tasks. They have less time to devote to complex or lengthy news stories and the economics of today's UK media sphere mean that fewer news outlets can afford large teams of investigative journalists and any investigations are necessarily time limited (Cairncross 2019). As Jim Waterson, media editor of *The Guardian* newspaper, commented,

> Simply for reasons of staffing, a British newspaper investigation will often mean that someone's spent no more than a couple of days on a story, and even that is a luxury that only big nationals and a couple of broadcasters can afford
>
> (participant 2) (See also Chapters 4 and 5).

Alongside data bombing, some organisations strategically provide the data requested by journalists or other researchers under Freedom of Information (FOI) requests in unsearchable formats. Such strategies may well be advised by an organisation's (in-house or agency) PR practitioners although the data trail to prove this would itself be very hard to research. As Stéphane Horel, an investigative journalist for *Le Monde* newspaper, described to me, some organisations will conform to the letter of the law by releasing documents when requested, but not in a format which can be easily searched and analysed. Rather, they release the information as images or photographs of texts which are far harder to analyse systematically (and software that translates such images into searchable text tends to insert errors). This is a significant issue for investigative journalists who are data bombed by organisations in the hope that they will be unable to find and analyse relevant information for any exposé that they are preparing.

As the above discussion makes clear, data bombing or snowing is a deliberate PR strategy designed to obscure and obstruct. But quite apart from such strategic mass releases of data, the super-abundance of publicly available information itself represents a challenge for individuals or groups wishing to filter out relevant issues or identify patterns. Rachel Oldroyd, former Managing Editor and CEO of the Bureau of Investigative Journalism, describes how this shift from discreet sources of data such as individual reports and files to mass digital resources has impacted on journalistic practice: 'it's not just brown paper envelopes or a box of paper that you've got to read through, you know, we're now getting... 900,000 documents that we need to try and work through digitally' (participant 36). As discussed in the next chapter, today's 'publicity' or 'transparency' of information has a complex relationship to secrecy and that which remains obscured or unintelligible.

'Astroturfing', front groups and the creation of counterfeit news stories

Another technique of secrecy deployed by PR – although it is certainly frowned upon in the industry as unethical – is 'astroturfing'. This is the creation of fake grassroots support for an issue, organisation or individual (Cave & Rowell 2014; Curry Jansen 2017; Miller & Dinan 2008; Shir-Raz & Avraham 2017; Stauber & Rampton 2004). In effect, it creates and circulates counterfeit public opinion in order to influence a particular issue. Jim Waterson, media editor of *The Guardian* newspaper, describes this PR practice in relation to planning applications: 'say a billionaire wanted to stop houses being developed next to his country retreat... he'd set up "Friends of the Chiltern Hills" pressure group and basically pay some PR to run it' (participant 2). Such a tactic aims to shortcircuit practices of public consultation while concealing the role that vested interests have taken in the attempts to manipulate the outcome of established processes. Astroturfing is related to another technique of disinformation – the creation of 'front groups': 'organizations with hidden agendas that deceptively present themselves as independent brokers of information or protectors of cherished social values, while concealing their true purposes and sources of funding' (Curry Jansen 2017: 103). Curry Jansen (2017: 104) gives the example of oil companies which have created front groups with names that evoke positive associations such as 'America's Wetland Foundation', and 'Women of the Storm' which were created after BP's 2010 Deepwater Horizon oil spill, the aim of which, Curry Jansen argues, was to 'shift the responsibility for the damage from corporations to taxpayers'. In relation to 'risk industries' such as alcohol or tobacco, other forms of front groups may reveal their source of funding but conceal their intentions, working to deflect further regulation of their industries and promoting personal responsibility over regulation, principles which sit well with the ideology of neoliberal capitalism (Pietracatella & Brady 2020).

Astroturfing and the creation of front groups are related to various PR reputation management techniques such as placing what appear to be news reports written by journalists on genuine news sites but which are, in fact, content created by PR practitioners that is placed on non-independent web sites. One of the PR practitioners in my study describes this practice while making it clear that his agency has never engaged in such practices. He notes,

> ... the increasing volume of websites and news outlets where you can publish your own content and then they're spending money distributing it by social media. So when we talk about fake news, this is something that I'm seeing more and more of – websites [on which] you're self-publishing your press releases and it aesthetically looks like a [genuine independent] news website... It's got the same font, the same pictures, the same sort of branding. If you self-publish something, you can pay extra for that self-published item to look even more like an editorial item by having a by-line or [the name of] a journalist on that article that *you've* written and *you've* submitted.
>
> (participant 8)

Rachael Levy (2019) gives the example of a businessman called Jacob Gottlieb who, when attempting to raise money for a hedge fund, employed a reputation management/PR firm called Status Labs[9] to improve his image online, as various unflattering or negative stories about him were circulating. Shortly after employing Status Labs, 'articles about him began to appear on websites that are designed to look like independent news outlets but are not. Most contained flattering information about Mr. Gottlieb, praising his investment acumen and philanthropy, and came up high in recent Google searches. Google featured some of the articles on Google News' (Levy 2019). Not only are such practices examples of Search Engine Optimisation (SEO) but highlight how PR practices can hijack and imitate the form and style of independent journalism in order to conceal or reframe issues that may impact negatively on clients.

Pre-emptive measures and 'preventive revelations'

PR concealment and media management techniques include temporal tactics that aim to pre-empt damaging disclosures of information to the media, or aim to anticipate and direct the public response to such damaging information. PR practitioners will advise their clients not only on their publicly oriented communications strategy but on their practices of internal communications: 'Internal public relations involves communicating with all of the organisation's employees – from the Board directors to casual labourers, from the newest recruit to staff with decades of experience, from administrative staff in head office to field forces based in overseas branches' (Moloney & McGrath 2020: 60). In the context of the United Kingdom's FOI legislation,[10] the portability of digital information and the potential for leaks and whistleblowing in an organisation, PR practitioners may advise their clients that they and their employees should avoid putting information or discussion in writing, including in reports, memos and emails (also see my discussion in Chapter 5). This is an attempt to manage the dynamics of secrecy and publicity by foreclosing the possibility of future disclosures of information. As one PR practitioner describes, 'people say, "oh please don't put that in an email, can you phone me instead to talk about this to make sure stuff doesn't come out?"' (participant 28). Such preventive secrecy techniques impact on the overall institutional culture and everyday practices of employees: 'if you think everything's going to be recorded, and therefore open to FOI requests, then you're not going to say what you think' (participant 13).

Such practices are part of a broader strategy of ensuring that 'plausible deniability' is built into organisations' practices and modes of communication, allowing organisations to deflect critical interest and conceal damaging issues by denying knowledge of them or responsibility for them. Plausible deniability can be mobilised alongside practices of 'strategic ignorance', which McGoey (2012: 570) argues can be seen as 'the deliberate effort to preclude, obfuscate or deflect knowledge from emerging' and can be advantageous as 'organizations often function more efficiently because of the shared willingness of individuals to band together in dismissing unsettling knowledge'.

'Preventive revelation' is another narrative management technique the aim of which is to 'get ahead of the story'.[11] Most PR media relations work is an attempt to shape the narrative and reception of a particular issue or story, but this technique of preventive revelation is rather more specific. In the event that PR practitioners think they will be unable to suppress the emergence of a negative issue about their client they may release to the media certain limited and carefully tailored information about the problematic issue, both via 'owned media' such as the organisation's web site and social media feeds and via press releases to secure the 'earned media' of journalists' reports. Knowing that fuller details about the damaging issue are likely to emerge, the PR practitioners will shortly after the first release of the limited information circulate more detail which includes the more damaging elements. The hope is that the public, or other interested parties such as regulators or investors, will merely note the updated story, and feel that as they are already aware of the issue having read the first version, they do not need to engage with the second (more damaging) story. A successful preventive revelation will enable PR practitioners to hide damaging information in plain sight while conforming to the principles of transparency.[12]

Sharp practice

Alongside the techniques of secrecy described above are a raft of practices which are generally seen as unethical in the PR industry – and may not be widely practiced – but which nevertheless figure in the arsenal of PR 'sharp practice'. As I discuss in more detail in Chapter 5, one of the milder tactics is the delaying of responses to FOI requests, often submitted by journalists. PR practitioners know that journalists are on tight schedules to submit their copy and that the shelf-life of a potential story is short, so delaying tactics can sometimes prevent a particular story from being written or published. PR practitioners may encourage clients to use Non-Disclosure Agreements (NDAs) to conceal inconvenient or damaging information, as well as to protect 'trade secrets'. This tactic is discussed in more detail in Chapter 4.

A more reprehensible tactic is the editing of online information about a client to present a more positive image, or as one PR practitioner puts it, 'to cynically manipulate [their image by] changing the Wikipedia entry' (participant 30).[13] There are PR/reputation management firms specialising in such practices, such as Wiki-PR[14] which promises to monitor and edit a client's Wikipedia entry, while claiming that such practices are legitimate and within the scope of Wikipedia's own guidelines. This is a tactic that attempts to actively erase or conceal certain information, as well as putting a positive gloss on a client's reputation. This technique may appeal when positive news stories may be difficult to place in the media through the traditional route of issuing press releases that are taken up by journalists. Another technique for managing adverse media coverage is discrediting the journalist who has written the negative story. As Brigitte Alfter, Director of the Arena for Journalism in Europe, notes, 'We see cases where journalists unveil something that is inconvenient... and we then see PR companies who are hired to smear these journalists and that's a very unpleasant aspect... because then PR is used to silence or to threaten to silence or to just make things to unpleasant so that [journalists] don't cover that topic anymore... it doesn't happen that frequently but it's nasty' (participant 38).

Expert opinion, third party endorsements and 'product defence companies'

Public relations can also orchestrate challenges to scientific evidence that inconveniently affects a particular sector, for instance, scientific findings about the environmental impact of a particular industry or the effects on human health of certain chemicals. David Michaels (2020, 2008), who served as Assistant Secretary of Labor for the Occupational Safety and Health Administration (OSHA) under Barack Obama from 2009 to 2017, and under Bill Clinton as Assistant Secretary of Energy for Environment, Safety and Health, has written exposés of what he calls this 'product defense industry': 'a cabal of apparent experts, PR flaks, and political lobbyists who use bad science to produce whatever results their sponsors want' (2020: 3). He describes the strategy of this industry – which includes PR practitioners – as one of 'manufacturing doubt' about scientific evidence in attempts to ward off regulation or lawsuits (Michaels 2020: 4).

> Studies in animals will be deemed irrelevant, human data are dismissed as not representative, and exposure data are discredited as unreliable. Always, there's too much doubt about the evidence, not enough proof of harm, not enough proof of enough harm. It is public relations disguised as science. The companies' PR experts provide these scientists with contrarian sound bites that play well with reporters, who are mired in the trap of believing there must be two sides to every story equally worthy of fair-minded consideration. The scientists are deployed to influence regulatory agencies that might be trying to protect the public, or to defend against lawsuits by people who believe they were injured by the product in question. The corporations and their hired guns market their studies and reports as 'sound science,' but actually they just sound like science. Such bought-and-paid-for corporate research is sanctified, while any academic research that might threaten corporate interests is vilified.
>
> Michaels (2020: 4)

In an interview with me, an investigative reporter who specialises in science writing comments on the product defence industry or what she refers to as 'scientific lobbying PR companies' which 'manipulate science to support lobbying' (Stéphane Horel, investigative journalist at *Le Monde* newspaper). She describes this as a very refined form of PR which aims to influence decision-makers, such as government or regulators. Her investigative reporting focuses on how they 'commission studies – scientists that are in the academic world or in specialised lobbying PR companies. There are specialised PR companies who work only with science matters and they employ people with… PhDs in the field to write… articles that will attack independent research showing harmful effects of [such a] chemical'. This journalist notes that she has researched the case of an elderly scientist who was paid to co-sign articles in significant scientific journals in order to cast doubt on the validity of other scientific evidence. The journalist states that the scientist revealed that he was paid only a modest sum which, the journalist argues, is because '[the industry] has to be careful not to give the impression they are buying people, especially if they approach a scientist in academia'. This use of 'third party endorsements', or in this case a third party critique, is an established PR practice and can be used across a range of industries and corporations, for example, in the pharmaceutical industry (see Shir-Raz & Avraham 2017).

It is hard to assess the extent and impact of such practices because the world of product defence companies is difficult to research. As Michaels writes, 'Secrets abound, and much of what we've learned comes from either lawsuits or, occasionally, careless mistakes in which donors are identified by accident' (2020: 11). But it is clear that specialist PR companies use experts to cast doubt on scientific findings for the benefit of vested interests and use journalism's commitment to offering 'balance' to a story – and journalists' desire for a scoop – to disseminate such ideas.

Creating the shadow world of the media sphere

This range of techniques of secrecy constitute the package that clients buy into when they engage PR as a promotional tool in order to secure positive publicity and to act as, in one PR practitioner's words, 'the protector of sensitive information' (participant 7). In this dual role, PR should be invisible if it is to function successfully – it is what Cutlip (1994) terms 'the unseen power': 'the PR should be behind the scenes. If people start seeing the spin and the PR then it's gone wrong somehow' (participant 28). This invisibility – of both the PR practices and the aspects of an organisation that the client wishes to remain obscure – is achieved in the creation of what I term the 'shadow world of the media sphere'. The PR industry's techniques of secrecy contribute to the constitution and maintenance of this shadow world in which well-resourced organisations, corporations and individuals can conceal information or practices that may be damaging to their reputation or which may attract unwelcome legal or regulatory attention. This shadow world not only conceals that which clients may wish to suppress but offers a virtual space – one which escapes the scrutiny of the news media, the public and the authorities – in which clients may strategise and consolidate their position. As Simmel (1906: 462) argues, this 'second world', or what I am calling the shadow world of the media sphere, is created by practices of secrecy and the particular character that the shadow world takes is shaped in any one culture or period by the specificities of those secrecy practices. In later chapters, I elaborate on how this shadow world is composed of shifting pockets of secrecy.

In the context that I am describing, PR's management and deployment of certain secrecy practices are today playing a significant and under-researched role. Practices such as encouraging clients to avoid putting into writing issues under discussion – in order to prevent leaks or to subvert potential FOI requests – create a shadow world within that organisation which is not legible to what Simmel (1906: 462) calls 'the obvious world'. Organisations' practices of data bombing or flooding the media sphere with information will give the appearance of transparency and open access to information while, in fact, creating a space in which issues that are potentially damaging to an organisation may hide in the midst of a distracting abundance of information. Diverting the public's scrutiny from an issue that is problematic for an organisation with an attention-grabbing but irrelevant story casts those damaging issues into shadow and draws the spotlight of media focus elsewhere.

However significant such targeted PR technologies of secrecy may be, PR has a more generalised and potentially more powerful relationship to secrecy and obfuscation. PR's creation of a shadow world conceals not only corporations' malfeasance or problematic issues that cast organisations in an unflattering light, it also hampers the public's or regulatory authorities' ability to achieve a fully informed understanding of how powerful interests operate and how society is shaped by the practices of those vested interests. The PR's industry efforts have the agglomerate effect of hampering 'joined up thinking' about the social world by offering disconnected units of information in press releases or on their client's web site or social media feeds, and skewing any released information as a positive promotional pitch. In this way, PR not only conceals how corporate power and organisational strategy operates, it impedes a wider systemic analysis of social relations. Simmel (1906) argues that in creating a second world (or shadow world, in my terms) secrecy impacts upon the 'obvious world', and it is clear how secrecy has a potent obfuscatory effect on the possibility of systematic critical thinking about the power relations of the social world.

These forms of distraction and concealment are not unambiguous 'lies' although they have a complex relationship to the truth. Simmel (1906: 445) argues that a lie is not a simple error in truth: the person to whom the lie is told is kept in the dark about the *intentions* of the liar, and hence secrecy is a fundamental element of the lie. This more expansive understanding of untruthfulness is helpful in revealing how PR impacts upon society. Its power resides not only in its capacity for factual manipulation or omission, nor in its various techniques of distraction and concealment. We can understand PR as 'untruth-full' in a broader and more insidious sense: its principles and practices act to conceal the intentions and strategic orientations of corporations and organisations, and PR obscures the ways in which the intentions and actions of its clients are interconnected in the wider context of capitalism.

Of course, most PR practice is far more pedestrian and much less nefarious than many of the techniques outlined in this chapter. Many PR practitioners would probably agree with one participant in my study who commented that most PR practice does not involve 'the dark arts' or 'spin doctors': 'a lot of the job is actually quite dry... it's about presenting the interests of your client in a way that... accentuates the positives and... tries to gloss over the negatives' (participant 27). PR does not attempt to present an objective picture. Its aim is not to be 'truthfull' but rather to be partial. In their strategic aim to promote the most positive image of a client, PR practitioners may present information that has only a tenuous connection to the truth. One PR practitioner notes, there is a temptation in PR work to, 'put out the things that aren't quite true but might be linked to a bit of truth' (participant 6), although PR practitioners recognise that this is a short-term and risky strategy as the truth will almost certainly be revealed eventually.

PR's role in supporting client interests in a partial way – partial as both non-objective and as selective – is unsurprising in a capitalist market system in which competition is the organising principle and brand image shapes the success of much competition (Brown 2015; Cronin 2018; Crouch 2011; Davies 2014; Piketty 2014). Equally, it is unsurprising that media reporting, fed and shaped by PR, often hampers or short-circuits more analytical and systematic understandings of the place of organisations' power in contemporary capitalism and the way in which power relations operate. This mirrors the way that journalism can contribute to 'media amnesia' in which news reports' lack of historical context and restricted range of perspectives can foreclose discussion of the wider picture and alternatives to current forms of capitalism (Basu 2018).

PR's social impact has been conceptualised in a range of ways, including as a form of propaganda with limited powers. As Moloney and McGrath argue, 'We see PR as the voice of rival interests, as weak propaganda, as the rhetorical manifestation of the structural power enjoyed by organisations and groups competing for social and economic advantage' (2020: 109). I agree that PR as a form of interest-driven communication can influence minds and shape attitudes. But secrecy practices in PR do more than attempt to change people's minds. As Simmel (1906) argues, secrecy actively *creates* social relations, shaping and maintaining social structures, institutions and processes. Moloney and McGrath (2020) suggest that PR can be seen as the rhetorical manifestation of organisations' and groups' power, and indeed there is ample evidence of this in the forms of brand communication it disseminates. Yet when PR practitioners engage in practices of publicity and secrecy, they are not simply reflecting the structural power of certain clients. Rather, they are tapping into more profound socially embedded practices and relationships that make up contemporary capitalism. As I explore in the following chapters, in playing on the secrecy–publicity dynamic that is woven into every society, the PR industry's engagement in communicative work acts to shape the particular forms that a society may take.

Notes

1 Public Affairs deals with managing external relations, such as attempting to exert influence on policy making, and includes areas such as political lobbying (see Cave & Rowell 2014; Davis 2002; Jackson & Moloney 2020).
2 The UK regulates lobbying through the Transparency of Lobbying, Non-Party Campaigning and Trade Union Administration Act (2014), although there is scepticism about its effectiveness at providing transparency (Parvin 2021; Solaiman 2021).
3 https://www.aboutamazon.co.uk/amazon-fulfilment/tour-an-amazon-fulfilment-centre. Accessed 28/1/22.
4 https://amazonuk.gcs-web.com/news-releases/news-release-details/donate-toy-amazon-uk-and-charity-kind-direct-delivering-smiles. Accessed 28/1/22.
5 https://ethicalmarketingnews.com/donate-a-toy-with-amazon-uk-and-charity-in-kind-direct-delivering-smiles-to-families-in-need-this-christmas. Accessed 28/1/22. Such web sites actively elicit contact from

companies to generate content. The 'Ethical Marketing' web page states, 'If you have a press release you would like us to feature then please contact us at: submissions@ethicalmarketingnews.com'. https://ethicalmarketingnews.com/aboutus.

6 See for example: https://www.theguardian.com/politics/2019/jun/26/mesmerising-boris-johnsons-bizarre-model-buses-claim-raises-eyebrows (accessed 19/1/22); https://www.mirror.co.uk/news/politics/boris-johnsons-bizarre-hobby-revealed-17211694 (accessed 19/1/22); https://www.huffingtonpost.co.uk/entry/boris-johnson-model-buses-hobby_uk_5d121740e4b0a3941868793d (accessed 19/1/22).

7 See https://www.bbc.co.uk/news/uk-politics-37167700 (accessed 28/1/22).

8 https://www.theguardian.com/politics/2016/aug/23/jeremy-corbyn-virgin-trains-disputes-claim-over-lack-of-seats. Accessed 28/1/22.

9 https://statuslabs.com/

10 Freedom of Information (FOI) legislation is relevant only for public bodies in the UK and excludes corporations.

11 For a more general account of 'preventive revelations' see Bratich (2007).

12 The danger of such revelations, of course, is that the negative information is placed (permanently) in the media sphere and is therefore available for journalists or the public to access at any point. However, as journalists are under such intense time pressure, their capacity to research stories in depth has diminished and therefore there is less danger in releasing the information in this managed form. As noted in the previous section, PR practitioners will also use Search Engine Optimisation (SEO) to push positive items to the top of the search results and bury more negative issues.

13 This is part of a wider phenomenon of online reputation management practices (see Draper 2020).

14 https://wiki-pr.com/.

References

Archer, C. (2019) 'Social media influencers, post-feminism and neoliberalism: How mum bloggers' 'playbour' is reshaping public relations', *Public Relations Inquiry*, 8(2): 149–166.

Basu, L. (2018) *Media Amnesia: Rewriting the Economic Crisis*. London: Pluto Press.

Bratich, J. (2007) 'Popular secrecy and occultural studies', *Cultural Studies*, 21(1): 42–58.

Brown, W. (2015) *Undoing the Demos: Neoliberalism's Stealth Revolution*. New York: Zone Books.

Brunner, B. R. (ed) (2019) *Public Relations Theory*. Hoboken, NJ: John Wiley & Son.

Cairncross, F. (2019) *The Cairncross Review: A Sustainable Future for Journalism*. https://assets.publishing.service.gov.uk/government/uploads/system/uploads/attachment_data/file/779882/021919_DCMS_Cairncross_Review_.pdf. Accessed 19/4/22.

Cave, T. & A. Rowell (2014) *A Quiet Word: Lobbying, Crony Capitalism, and Broken Politics in Britain*. London: The Bodley Head.

Coco, S. L. and S. Eckert (2020) '#sponsored: Consumer insights on social media influencer marketing', *Public Relations Inquiry*, 9(2): 177–194.

Cronin, A. M. (2018) *Public Relations Capitalism: Promotional Culture, Publics and Commercial Democracy*. Cham: Palgrave Macmillan.

Crouch, C. (2011) *The Strange Non-death of Neoliberalism*. Cambridge, MA: Polity.

Curry Jansen, S. (2017) *Stealth Communication: The Spectacular Rise of Public Relations*. Cambridge, MA & Malden, MA: Polity.

Cutlip, S. M. (1994) *The Unseen Power: Public Relations, A History*. Hillsdale, NJ: Erlbaum Associates.

Davies, C. & M. Hobbs (2020) 'Irresistible possibilities: Examining the uses and consequences of social media influencers for contemporary public relations', *Public Relations Review*, 46(5): 2020. doi.org/10.1016/j.pubrev.2020.101983.

Davies, W. (2014) *The Limits of Neoliberalism: Authority, Sovereignty and the Logic of Competition*. London: Sage.

Davis, A. (2002) *Public Relations Democracy*. Manchester: Manchester University Press.

Draper, N. A. (2020) 'Metaphors of visibility: rhetorical practices in the normalization of individual online image management', *American Behavioral Scientist*, 64(11): 1627–1645.

Edwards, L. (2018) *Understanding Public Relations: Theory, Culture and Society*. London: Sage.

L'Etang, J. (2008) *Public Relations: Concepts, Practice, Critique*. London: Sage.

Levy, R. (2019) 'How the 1% Scrubs Its Image Online – Prominent figures from Wall Street to Washington received help from a firm that buries sensitive Google results', *Wall Street Journal*, 14 December. http://proquest.umi.com/login/athens?url=https://www.proquest.com/newspapers/exchange-how-1-scrubs-image-online-prominent/docview/2325697425/se2?accountid=11979. Accessed 12/1/22.

McGoey, L. (2012) 'The logic of strategic ignorance', *The British Journal of Sociology*, 63: 533–576.

McIntyre, N. (2022) 'Fossil fuel firms among biggest spenders on Google ads that look like search results', *The Guardian*, 5 January. https://www.theguardian.com/technology/2022/jan/05/fossil-fuel-firms-among-biggest-spenders-on-google-ads-that-look-like-search-results? Accessed 6/1/21

Michaels, D. (2020) *The Triumph of Doubt: Dark Money and the Science of Deception*, Oxford & New York: Oxford University Press.

Michaels, D. (2008) *Doubt Is Their Product: How Industry's Assault on Science Threatens Your Health*. Oxford & New York: Oxford University Press.

Miller, D. & W. Dinan (2008) *A Century of Spin: How Public Relations Became the Cutting Edge of Corporate Power*. London: Pluto Press.

Moloney, K. & C. McGrath (2020) *Rethinking Public Relations: Persuasion, Democracy and Society* (3rd ed). London & New York: Routledge.

Munshi, D, & P. Kurian (2020) *Public Relations and Sustainable Citizenship: Representing the Unrepresented.* London & New York: Routledge.

Parvin, P. (2021) 'UK lobbying rules explained: why no one seems to be in legal trouble', *The Conversation*, 27 April. https://theconversation.com/uk-lobbying-rules-explained-why-no-one-seems-to-be-in-legal-trouble-159741. Accessed 18/1/22.

Pietracatella, R. & D. Brady (2020) 'A new development in front group strategy: the social aspects public relations organization (SAPRO)', *Frontiers in Communication*, 5(24). https://doi.org/10.3389/fcomm.2020.00024

Piketty, T. (2014) *Capital in the Twenty-First Century.* Cambridge, MA: Harvard University Press.

Schultheiß, S. & D. Lewandowski (2021) '"Outside the industry, nobody knows what we do": SEO as seen by search engine optimizers and content providers', *Journal of Documentation*, 77(2): 542–557.

Shir-Raz, Y. & E. Avraham (2017) '"Under the regulation radar": PR strategies of pharmaceutical companies in countries where direct advertising of prescription drugs is banned—the Israeli case', *Public Relations Review*, 43(2): 382–391.

Simmel, G. (1906) 'The sociology of secrecy and of secret societies', *American Journal of Sociology*, 11(4): 441–498.

Solaiman, B. (2021) 'Lobbying in the UK: towards robust regulation', *Parliamentary Affairs*, gsab051, https://doi.org/10.1093/pa/gsab051

Stauber, J.C. and S. Rampton (2004) *Toxic Sludge Is Good For You: Lies, Damn Lies and the Public Relations Industry.* London: Robinson.

Stohl, C., M. Stohl & P.M. Leonardi (2016) 'Managing opacity: information visibility and the paradox of transparency in the digital age', *International Journal of Communication,* 10: 123–137.

Visser, W., D. Matten, M. Pohl, M, & N. Tolhurst (2010) *The A to Z of Corporate Social Responsibility* (2nd ed). Somerset: Wiley.

4 News cultures, journalism and the secrecy–publicity dynamic

An analysis of the relationship between public relations and journalism is key to understanding the operation of both secrecy and publicity in the media sphere as well as the dynamic relation of the secrecy–publicity nexus. As outlined in the previous chapter, one of PR's tasks is to conceal or de-emphasise any negatively inflected stories or information about its clients, or to outweigh such adverse publicity by creating positively inflected narratives. One of journalism's core tasks is to investigate issues, uncover the actions of vested interests, reveal information and create narratives that facilitate the clear communication of what has been uncovered. At first glance PR and journalism appear to operate as binaries that pivot neatly on the fulcrum of secrecy–publicity: one attempts to reveal while the other attempts to conceal or dissemble. There is certainly a close, and some would say symbiotic, relationship between PR and journalism: journalism provides much of the mainstream news media context into which PR attempts to insert its promotional narratives, and some sectors of journalism rely increasingly on PR material such as press releases in order to generate news content (Cronin 2018; Forde & Johnston 2013; Franklin 2010; Gandy 1982; Jackson and Moloney 2016; Lewis et al. 2008a, 2008b; Macnamara 2016; McChesney 2012; Phillips 2010).[1]

However, rather than figuring PR as a social technology of secrecy and obfuscation, and journalism as a social technology of revelation and transparency, it is important to recognise the complexities of each industry's relationship to the secrecy–publicity dynamic. As I have argued, PR practices are oriented to both publicity *and* secrecy and, as I will explore in this and the next chapter, journalism's relationship to secrecy is multi-layered and ambivalent. Both PR and journalism in the United Kingdom are structured by wider socially embedded discourses and practices of secrecy and publicity, such as Non-Disclosure Agreements (NDAs), the Official Secrets Act, Freedom of Information

DOI: 10.4324/9781003369585-4

(FOI) legislation, lobbying regulation, codes of practice, institutional norms and organisational cultures. These discourses and practices are anchored in social and legal systems and financial models, and act to shape the specific character of the secrecy–publicity dynamic as it manifests in the United Kingdom today. As Simmel (1906) argues, the particular ways that secrecy and publicity are practiced will impact upon the form of social relations and the very structure of society in any one period and culture. In effect, the practices and ideas associated with secrecy and publicity are generative and they generate, among other things, a shadow world of the media sphere.

This chapter explores how the relationship between journalism and PR is shaped by secrecy–publicity and, in turn, how that relationship acts to shape the media sphere. In what follows I draw on my interview material, case studies and a range of data and academic sources to offer a brief outline of the field of UK journalism today, a discussion of the relationship between journalism and PR, and an analysis of two key technologies of secrecy that shape PR and journalistic practice and influence generally circulating ideas about media secrecy: Non-Disclosure Agreements (NDAs) and DSMA-Notices.

UK journalism today

My aim here is to signal some characteristics of UK news culture and changes in the field of journalism that are relevant to my specific focus on secrecy and publicity, rather than offer a comprehensive review of the rich literature on news culture. I highlight the interface between journalism and PR and explore its significance for shaping the field of news and for understanding how secrecy and publicity operate in the media today.

It has been widely recognised that UK journalism and news cultures are undergoing major changes and facing profound challenges. The report published by the government-commissioned Cairncross Review (2019) summarises many of these shifts, including the financial pressures placed on many news outlets by the declining revenue derived from advertising.

> [w]hile both the transition to smartphones and the nature of the online advertising market have made it much harder for news publishers to generate advertising revenue, the fundamental problem with their scale strategy is that, even with much larger reach, the advertising space news publishers sell is simply not valuable enough. There are too many alternative advertising opportunities

available across the internet. If news publishers are to raise more revenue from online advertising, they must find ways to make their advertising space more valuable.

(Cairncross 2019: 44)

The expansion of digital content has also impacted on the public's expectations which place further pressure on news outlets, as one PR practitioner noted, 'consumers want content for free, but somehow it has to be paid for' (participant 11). Technological developments and a growing 'platformization' of the media sphere (Van Dijck et al. 2018) have transformed news and PR cultures, and many people today encounter news incidentally while using social media (Fletcher & Nielsen 2018). For instance, there has been a dramatic growth in the number and influence of media agencies which digitise, track and commodify media audiences, channelling them towards certain news media outlets (Willig 2022). In parallel, the work practices of media professionals such as journalists and PR practitioners have been transformed (Bourne 2022). There has been a major shift in the gatekeeping role of journalists facilitated by the expansion of social media and the platform this provides the public to respond to news stories (including contributing images, tip offs, etc.), circulate certain perspectives on current affairs, debate issues and indeed create their own reports. As Alan Rusbridger, former editor of *The Guardian* newspaper, told me,

I suppose the enormous change is from a distribution method which was one-way, and in which people were very restricted in their access to information, and journalists were the only gatekeepers in the world, to one in which anybody can be a publisher, anybody can respond, there are a multiplicity of sources... the switch from paper to digital [newspapers] was obviously a big thing, but I think the move from digital to social [media] is the major thing.

The financial pressures faced by news outlets have led to a reduction in the number of journalists employed and an increase in the workload of the remaining journalists.[2] This trend has been exacerbated by today's 24/7 news cycle which has increased pressures on journalists to produce new content and update stories in real time. When once journalists would file their stories at set points, with perhaps one later update required, journalists must now produce news stories almost constantly (Waisbord & Russell 2020; also see Le Cam and Domingo's (2015) study of online newsrooms in France and Spain). This time pressure, and increased demand for content, appears to have reduced the depth of the coverage of events (Lewis et al. 2005). Waisbord and Russell suggest that the rapid production of short news reports may also be shaped by 'the increasingly short attention span of publics. In information ecologies with huge attention inequalities, any news is likely to receive limited, brief journalistic and public attention' (2020: 380). The time pressures may also reduce the accuracy of that reporting. As Alan Rusbridger commented, journalists 'don't have time to do any interviewing sometimes... [they have to produce]... eight stories in a day, ten stories in a day, and you can't do any sort of proper checking of those stories if you're basically just churning stuff out'.

Another change that impacts on the work of both journalists and PR practitioners is the vast quantity of data that circulates publicly today. Participants in my study commented that this provides both a challenge and an opportunity. Jim Waterson, media editor of *The Guardian* newspaper, described how the availability of data can assist in researching stories:

> Things are definitely getting easier [because of] the amount of data that's around pretty much through a Google search from reputable sources.... If you want to find out the official government stats on onion exports [for example], then I bet if you went onto Google right now and typed 'UK government exports, onions', you'd probably quite quickly find yourself on a Defra[3] dataset that had that information you needed within three minutes. That's clearly fantastic for when you're doing a fast turnaround profile on British agriculture after Brexit.

But the abundance of data also generates difficulties, such as identifying and analysing relevant information. A former newspaper and broadcast journalist commented on the problems this raises and the relatively new phenomenon of 'data journalists[4] who have the technical skills to manipulate and analyse complex datasets:

> ... there is just tonnes of blooming information available. It's a question of finding it, processing it, understanding it. So that's beyond a lot of people and it's beyond a lot of journalists... data journalism, data sorting... you need to know what you're doing there. So... there is a lot of [data] available but have people got the time and the expertise to actually make sense of it and dig out what's in there?
>
> (participant 1)

The use of data in journalism, however, does not necessarily produce enhanced coverage of a story. As Cushion et al. (2017: 1211) argue, 'data – in the form of statistical references – does indeed inform a considerable share of everyday news coverage, although often with little context or detail'.

Another characteristic of UK news culture today is the declining investment in investigative reporting which is directly related to the troubled finances of the field. The Cairncross Review (2019: 7) identified investigative journalism as one of the areas of journalism that is 'most worthy and most under threat'.

> Investigative journalism is easily the riskiest and most expensive activity that most publishers undertake…. Such journalism presents an enormous challenge, but it is also at the heart of the journalist's role as guardian of public probity…. Do newspapers recoup the costs of producing such stories with extra readers? The Review has seen no evidence on this; rather… it seems likely that much investigative journalism is undertaken by the mainstream press as an investment in reputation. There may be direct rewards in a digital world: one online journalist told the Review that people spent longer reading investigative news, which made it more valuable to advertisers. However, advertising revenue generated by the article is unlikely to approach anywhere near the cost of creating that content in the first place. Thus, if the transition to digital and a consequent decline in publishers' revenues is likely to reduce the supply of good investigative journalism, the public has an interest in finding ways to support it.
>
> (Cairncross 2019: 19)

The increased pressure placed on journalists who cover daily news stories to produce ever more stories can also impact on the time and resources that news outlets can devote to investigative journalism. Rachel Oldroyd, former Managing Editor and CEO of the Bureau of Investigative Journalism, describes the significance of this interrelationship:

> For the rest of the news teams who are… on daily newsbeats… we're now in 24/7, you have to be reporting all the time and that's a very different skill. But that has also had a massive impact on the rest of the industry 'cos it… sucks up a huge amount of resource and money and that takes time, resource and focus off the longer term… bigger investigative work'.

This perspective was supported by all the journalists in my study. One effect has been a stronger demarcation between investigative journalism and daily news journalism, as Richard Sambrook, former BBC editor (and former PR practitioner), commented:

> The workload has gone up significantly and I suppose at one level [journalism has] become much more of a kind of processing task, information processing, than... information uncovering or gathering, so the investigative news function has changed significantly. There's still quite a lot of investigative journalism going on, but it is very much a specialist function in a way that you know 30, 40 years ago any journalist might decide to do an investigative story alongside whatever else they were doing. Well, they don't have the time for that now. These roles have become... separated out... with a lot of deadlines and so on you're always on 24/7 news schedules. So people are feeding that machine or they're outside of that trying to do a different kind of long-form investigative, specialist journalism.

The combined impact of such challenges to journalism and news culture has led many journalists and editors to express grave concerns about, 'a massive hollowing out of newsrooms across the country and particularly expensive journalists and expensive journalism, which is investigative journalism' (Rachel Oldroyd, participant 36). Curran describes what he considers to be the decline of news media, remarking that 'legacy news media have not been dethroned. But newspapers have haemorrhaged revenue, depleting their quality and coverage' (Curran 2022: 46). Of particular concern is the decline in public interest reporting, as the Cairncross Review notes: 'as the digital transition has led most publishers to cut costs, the provision of public interest news has been weakened' (Cairncross 2019: 77). The problems faced by journalism and news culture today offer opportunities for PR and its clients, shifting the power relations in the media sphere.

The shifting relationship between journalism and PR

The relationship between journalism and PR in the United Kingdom has evolved over the years in response to the various factors described above. As outlined in previous chapters, the PR industry in many countries has expanded significantly with more organisations employing either in-house or agency PR practitioners to manage their relationship with the public and external bodies (as well as internal communications). In the United Kingdom, this leads to an intensive targeting of journalists by PR practitioners, a trend exacerbated by the reduction in the overall number of journalists. As one journalist in my study noted, 'I get emails by PRs like maybe 50 or 60 times a day... most of the time it's just mass mailouts.... I've [clearly] been added to a list about stuff that I have absolutely no interest in' (participant 26). This mass mailout technique, known in the PR industry as 'spray and pray', rarely connects with journalists in the way that PR practitioners may hope and indeed most in my study recognised that. It has another key impact, however, in that it contributes significantly to the intense circulation of information and communications in the media sphere, feeding the sense identified by Dean (2002) that there must be yet more information to be revealed.

The growth of the PR industry has also impacted upon journalists' practices by creating a mediating buffer between journalists and the sources they wish to access. Journalists in my study stated that this was a striking change:

> When I studied journalism in the 1990s we could call any organisation, government, or commercial organisation and it was really easy to get through to the people who actually were working with a particular matter or project or case. And over the 1990s into the 2000s this ended because there is a huge layer of spokespersons and people that were employed to [manage] journalists, so it's really hard to get to the first sources, to the officials or the employees in companies who actually work with the question that I'm interested in.
>
> (Brigitte Alfter, Director of the Arena for Journalism in Europe, participant 38)

> When I started out at the *Barking Advertiser* in East London, the council didn't have PR. I mean, you just spoke to the council – you spoke to the officers, the town clerk, or his assistant.... There was just no filter.... So that's the biggest change – the creation of barriers between journalists and their targets.
>
> (Roy Greenslade, participant 20)

PR practitioners' intermediary role means that they have more control over journalists' access to their clients, and over shaping stories and de-emphasising negative aspects of issues relating to their clients. The growth of the PR industry's influence also fuels journalists' perception that they must intensify their efforts to peel away the veneer created by PR communications in order to reveal the truth beneath: 'you have a lot of resource and effort going into managing the public [PR] message about all sorts of things. You've got to get beyond [that] to find out what's really going on' (Eliot Higgins, Director of Bellingcat, an open source investigations collective, participant 35). Yet because UK journalism is increasingly poorly resourced, and there are fewer journalists to cover more work, PR messaging can be taken up and used as news content by journalists under pressure with very few checks or little rewriting of the material. It has long been the case that PR press releases and PR-managed interviews and events have acted as 'information subsidies' for journalists, providing conveniently packaged material for use as content in news reports (Gandy 1982). This was famously described by Nick Davies (2009) as part of a culture of 'churnalism' in which news stories are produced in large number and at speed. But it has been suggested that this trend has intensified in various countries to the degree that PR practitioners are now offering 'editorial subsidies' – in effect, fully prepared reports tailored to each media outlet which could be published with no journalistic input or editorial changes (Boumans 2018; Cronin 2018; Forde & Johnston 2013; Jackson & Moloney 2016; Lewis et al. 2008; McChesney 2012; Phillips 2010). This may be particularly prevalent in specialist areas such as science communication (see Williams & Gajevic 2013). Alan Rusbridger, former editor of *The Guardian* newspaper, commented on the development of this trend:

> I think the penny dropped [in the PR industry] that as newsrooms became hollowed out, journalists were increasingly dependent on being fed stuff [through press releases]... the amount of stuff that just... went almost un-rewritten straight into the paper!... Just giving it a sort of spurious veneer of having been news that's been processed. So once [the PR industry] cottoned onto that, then PR became even bigger.

Another very experienced journalist summarises the impact of the various shifts in news media culture and the related growth in influence of PR:

> What has happened is that with the advent of the internet and the creation of platforms like Google and Facebook... the decline in print circulation has greatly increased and that's partly as a result of a very strategic error in my view that was made by newspapers generally about 15, 20 years ago which was to effectively put the vast majority of the material they generate free online. So they conditioned people to expect to get information free of charge and that's created enormous problems because the business model... is predicated on replacing lost print revenue with increased digital revenue and essentially it's never going to happen. So you've got a situation where there is constant cuts, which lead to far fewer

people working in the industry... than there used to be the case, and that's had a huge knock-on effect in terms of the quality of material which is published because there's a lot of pressure to fill the space and that has made it easier for organisations which want to get their point across to use PR in order to put things into print. And so there's far less time around now for investigative journalism of the old style, and a lot of the material which is published is very superficial. They talk about ludicrous preoccupations... for example, with silly stories about Wetherspoons and Greggs' pasties, and one of the reasons why they do it is because it's the lowest common denominator and they get lots of clicks. But also, of course, it's effectively reproducing a company press release [which] is far easier and far less challenging than actually holding local power brokers to account.

(Martin Shipton, participant 3)

The decline of investment in journalism has other advantages for the media relations sector of the PR industry. As intermediaries for their clients, PR practitioners – and the PR messaging they produce – are now much less likely to be scrutinised with any intensity by overstretched journalists. One PR practitioner commented,

I don't get a hard time [from journalists] like I used to.... There were certain journalists in the past [when] you'd see their [phone] number come up, and your skin would go cold... You knew that either they knew something that you didn't, which would put you on the backfoot straight away, or they were going to you [to ask] something and you knew it was tricky, and you were going to have to step extremely carefully... because they either had a very challenging view of what you were doing and were going to put you under a degree of scrutiny and your organisation [under] a degree of scrutiny. It doesn't happen [now] as much.

(participant 7)

The picture painted of the changes in United Kingdom, and indeed Euro-American, journalism by my respondents and by much of the academic literature, is very negative in its implications for civic culture and democracy (see Curran 2022; Gans 2003; Media Reform Coalition 2021; Reese 2021; Schudson 2018). Some commentators, such as Moloney and McGrath (2020: 86), believe that, 'journalism's complicity with PR and its information subsidies has now become virtual capitulation'. One journalist's remarks capture the dominant view amongst journalists and editors in my study: he commented that it is a very worrying situation, 'from the point of view of democracy because it means that we have a public that is far less well-informed than they deserve to be. So I think that it has serious dangers' (Martin Shipton, participant 3).

However, the challenges faced by journalism today do not *always* translate into advantages for PR. As various of my respondents noted, in the past it may have been easier for some PR practitioners to succeed in efforts to suppress a story by drawing on their long-established and trusting relationships with journalists. One speculates that this may still be possible for some PR practitioners through 'old boys' networks' (participant 28). With the advent of social media networks, citizen journalism, open source media investigation groups such as Bellingcat, and enhanced opportunities for whistleblowers to disseminate information, suppressing a story is now far more challenging for the PR industry and even temporary successes rarely translate into long-term concealment of a problematic issue. The 24/7 news cycle and the growth of internet news sites, which presents such challenges for journalists, may in some ways offer opportunities for media relations PR: as noted above, more news content is required and, therefore, PR can potentially secure more media coverage for clients by offering their press releases and pre-prepared material to journalists. But the speed of the news cycle means that PR can struggle to respond adequately or to strategically 'get ahead of the story':

> The 24/7 [news cycle] actually, bizarrely, has had a slight push back on PR because [journalists] are reporting on news that is happening at that moment and even PR can't operate that quickly.... If you see the stories that lead the news agenda they do tend to be... the breaking news stories that PR can't feed into in the same way as it used to feed into daily reporting.
>
> (Rachel Oldroyd, former Managing Editor & CEO of the Bureau of Investigative Journalism, participant 36)

The relationship between journalism and PR – and that relationship's interface with the dynamics of secrecy–publicity – is shifting and complex. As I have described it is shaped by transformations in media finance and the affordances of communications technologies. But those relationships are also shaped by key socio-legal institutions and practices.

Social technologies of secrecy: media and legal governance

While PR may wield considerable 'soft power' by negotiating the opportunities provided by both secrecy and publicity in the media sphere, some of the other key ways that organisations or individuals manage to suppress damaging news stories are based in law. PR techniques for suppressing or diminishing the negative impact of stories are different from legal procedures for attempting to suppress stories, but as I discuss in this and the next chapter, both sets of practices share the fact that they are situated within a wider secrecy–publicity dynamic. In their description of their encounters with both lawyers and PR practitioners, an investigative journalist captures a theme that emerged many times in my study:

> I've never come across an instance in which a PR person attempts to suppress a story. What will happen is that the PR person's boss sometimes decides to try to suppress the story but they will tend to do that through lawyers and the lawyers will start issuing threats.... If you have a hammer everything looks like a nail. If you're a lawyer, the immediate problem in front of you is something to sue, whereas if you're a PR person your instinct is to issue a statement about it. And so my general experience of working with investigations into corporate bodies is that the PR person will often just give you a statement. I've not had one where they try to stop us from writing about it, you know, unless it was... leaked material... but again that ends up being a legal dispute, it's not a PR thing.
>
> (participant 33)

While I did find evidence of PR practitioners attempting to suppress stories through a range of techniques (counter to the experience of the journalist above), the use of the law to suppress negative news stories or the circulation of damaging information is clearly a standard corporate or institutional practice. The same journalist describes how secrecy practices operate in investigative journalism:

> Oftentimes the challenge of secrecy doesn't come at the time we're researching it, it comes at the time when we go to [them for a] comment, because that's the point at which they instruct solicitors who say 'you can't publish *that*, you can't publish *that*, you can't

publish *that* and if you do we'll sue you'. At which point you then get into a negotiation with your own lawyers and your own editors and you have to work out what your organisation is willing to publish. That's the point at which secrecy becomes the game you're playing.

(participant 33)

One journalist gave the example of being threatened by a PR practitioner in relation to a particular section of a story they had written about a large corporation. They describe their dismay when their employer, a national UK newspaper, decided that the risk of threatened legal action outweighed the benefits of publishing that particular element of the story:

I obviously fed back to my editors at [a national newspaper] [that x corporation] is being very aggressive and is threatening to sue us about this line in the piece and they were like, 'right, we'll just take it out', which I found really disappointing 'cos I knew that the line was accurate but [the legal threat] worked…. The [national newspaper] was, like, 'we don't really want to get sued for this thing that's not that essential to the piece so we'll just take it out.'

(participant 26)

The journalist noted that although the legal device had worked in terms of suppressing the specific claim they had made in the original piece, the tactic had had a negative longer term effect as it shaped their view of that corporation: 'it was also terrible PR because [the company's PR contact] was so rude to me that I will literally never write another favourable article about [x corporation] ever again and I told the entire [national newspaper] […] desk how… he spoke to me. He was so condescending and so incredibly rude' (participant 26). In this case, the actions of that PR practitioner established long-term poor relations with this national newspaper. Those actions also set in place tensions between the corporation's secrecy practices and the potential for journalists to push hard for future revelations as retaliation for their treatment.

The Guardian newspaper's media lawyer, Gill Phillips (2021), comments on how those with the resources to pay top legal teams are able to police what is published in the media sphere: 'The rich, the famous and the powerful don't like criticism and don't like having their dirty laundry aired in public. They can be well-resourced, and will spend heavily on expensive lawyers'. She describes the legal process that is triggered when a journalist produces a story containing sensitive information:

> ... the journalists will put together any 'right to reply' letters that will be sent out seeking comment from those who may be criticised. Once those letters go out, we can usually expect to get a barrage of responses, often from expensive claimant-friendly lawyers, some of whom are hired to try to put journalists off publishing, usually by whatever means they can – threats, bluster, as well as, where appropriate, pointing out that we have misunderstood something or missed a key bit of evidence.
>
> (Phillips 2021)

Phillips notes that the costs of fighting a legal case to trial in the United Kingdom are very high for a news outlet and, even if they won, there may well be legal costs to pay. Clients' perception of the benefits of hiring lawyers to protect information and their reputation may be shaped by the national context: 'London is considered by some as the libel capital of the world, and many use English lawyers to silence their critics. Because we publish via a website, where anyone can access and read our stories, we face the possibility of being sued anywhere in the world' (Phillips 2021). The legal power of such well-resourced organisations, and the practice of what Leigh (2019: 78) calls 'legal bullying', may well have a chilling effect on journalism. One journalist in my study noted the related use of 'SLAPP suits' (Strategic Lawsuit Against Public Participation) by powerful interests wishing to suppress certain information[5] (see, for example, Hilson 2016; Murphy & Moerman 2018). There is evidence of widespread use of SLAPP suits, or vexatious lawsuits, against journalists and news organisations, causing considerable concern among journalists (Selva 2020). These are, in effect, legal threats issued by well-funded interested parties. The instigator of a SLAPP suit may not expect to win the legal case should it go to court, but this is not the point – the aim of issuing the threat is to intimidate an organisation or individual (such as a news outlet or a journalist) into not publicising certain information.

UK law frames the possibilities for well-resourced bodies to manage the publication or release of damaging information and creates a particular culture that restricts public access to information. Robert Phillips, who has long worked in PR and is now a vocal critic of many of the industry's principles and practices, commented that even when some company CEOs may be open to a degree of transparency – and to offering more information to the public through PR routes – they are advised by their lawyers not to release certain information: 'actually, it's become... more intensified over the past three or four years. Lawyers are a huge part of the problem, so even when you had a willing CEO – to be transparent about a certain situation – the legal advice would be, "no, you can't say that. You mustn't say that. That might lead to liability or lead to risk"' (participant 16). Caution may, therefore, lead companies to restrict the information that is made publicly available and to threaten journalists and news outlets with legal action should certain stories be published.

This culture of legal risk and caution may be internalised by news editors and stitched into editorial practices with the result that some news outlets may become more timid about publishing certain controversial stories, although there are many counter-examples of bold journalistic coverage of controversial areas discussed in the next chapter. My aim in the above section has not been to provide an exhaustive account of media law. My point is that the relationship between media coverage (publicity) and the techniques deployed by organisations to achieve secrecy is shaped not only by PR practice but by legal strictures (which themselves inform PR practices). Other legal technologies of secrecy that intersect with both journalistic and PR practice are Non-Disclosure Agreements (NDAs) and DSMA-Notices.

Non-Disclosure Agreements and DSMA-Notices as technologies of secrecy

Confidentiality agreements/clauses are commonly known as Non-Disclosure Agreements (NDAs) or 'gagging orders'. They can be used to protect intellectual property rights or to control the flow of information in a range of instances, such as employer/employee disputes. The Law Society describes the objectives and parameters of NDAs:

> They prevent employees from making business secrets and sensitive information public or sharing them with competitors.... They're also often contained in settlement agreements, which allow an employer and employee to resolve a workplace dispute confidentially without going to a tribunal or court. Confidentiality clauses can place legal restrictions on you.... Confidentiality clauses are not legally binding if they try to stop you talking to the police or a regulator about issues between you and your employer or someone at work. An agreement may not be legally binding if you're not given reasonable time to think about it and/or get

independent legal advice before signing it. Confidentiality clauses cannot be used to stop whistleblowing (telling your employer or someone else about anything illegal or dangerous you know is happening at work) in the public interest.[6]

As one PR practitioner in my study puts it, NDAs are used 'so that things don't come out' (participant 28) (see also Costas & Grey 2016). They have been considered 'a weapon of epistemic violence' (Pagan 2021: 302) which aims to exert power through silencing. I argue that NDAs can also be understood as a social technology of secrecy.

Although it is hard to determine their prevalence in the United Kingdom, many of the PR, journalist and editor participants in my study had experience of them in their everyday practice. Alan Rusbridger remarked that NDAs were one of the many ways that organisations have found to suppress information which makes it challenging for journalists to hold those organisations to account. One journalist commented that not only was their use widespread but they can offer financial benefits for those who agree to sign them, either as part of their standard employment contract or at the point that they leave the organisation:

> [NDAs] happen a lot and I think it's quite shocking that there are Non-Disclosure Agreements particularly in the public sector which still exist.... Years ago, the [high ranking official] in [a governmental body] ... actually made a statement... to the effect that they didn't use Non-Disclosure Agreements. But, I mean, that was completely untrue because I was aware of instances where Non-Disclosure Agreements had been offered to people and they were told if you sign this Non-Disclosure Agreement then we will give you more money. And [they are used] as a severance payment.
>
> (Martin Shipton, participant 3)

Some PR practitioners in my study noted that various sections of an organisation, including legal advisors, can collaborate in order to conceal damaging issues and bolster the organisation's reputation:

> ... it's that kind of work in-between the lawyers and HR and PR and when you've got those people round the table, it's quite scary actually what an organisation could look at trying to hide.... We've seen some of the big scandals like #MeToo where things are hidden because you get people to sign NDAs.
>
> (participant 28)

The same individual notes that not all PR practitioners are willing to sign NDAs or conceal information, a refusal which sometimes costs them their jobs: 'I've heard stories about PR people... having to leave their jobs because of not wanting to cover things up. I've heard stories about people having to sign NDAs to cover up stories, being paid off' (participant 28). While it is hard to corroborate such accounts, there appears to be ample evidence of the widespread use of NDAs and financial inducements to manage the flow of information and mitigate the risks of reputational damage in the media sphere.[7] The affordances provided by the internet and digital culture more generally mean that information can escape controls and circulate more easily (Couldry & Hepp 2016) and this itself may generate more interest from organisations in the preventive potential of NDAs. A PR practitioner who had worked in-house for a large film corporation for many years comments on how corporations will attempt to protect commercially valuable information through the use of NDAs for staff members (including the in-house PR practitioners):

> Information just spreads so much quicker. It's such a commodity now.... Every YouTuber or blogger out there, let alone journalists who are paid to do it, [are searching for] any scrap they can get of a release date... a leaked picture.... Film makers believed that those kind of leaks impact the success of the films.... They took it incredibly seriously, you know, it's corporate theft.... It's led to NDAs being [used] more and more.... People have had their fingers burnt so much.... All the film studios have leaks all the time, you know, from extras on set who could sneak a phone in and take a picture of something, through to maybe blueprints of products leaking.
>
> (participant 31)

NDAs can, therefore, be used as a tool for managing information escape from employees in both private and public sector organisations, but they can also be used more generally as a means of suppressing information. As a social technology of secrecy, NDAs have the effect of making journalists' task of uncovering and publishing information more difficult. One investigative journalist employed by a UK national newspaper commented that NDAs are used as a form of intimidation and they hamper his task of accessing information from sources who are unsure about what they may safely reveal:

> I'm so deeply cynical about [NDAs]. It's because.... I spend my entire life dealing with threats from lawyers who say that they're

going to sue [journalists and newspapers] and then don't. It's just
bluff, of course. NDAs are an extension of that to normal people.
It's designed to threaten people. It's designed to make you think,
'Am I going to get sued if I cross the line? Where is the line? I don't
really know – I better just shut up'. It feels to me [that it's] a tactic
of intimidation.

(participant 33)

The use of NDAs may intersect with other PR tactics that are oriented to protecting or repairing the reputation of an organisation,
either proactively as an ongoing media strategy or in response to a
specific crisis that threatens an organisation's public image. For instance, media attention has been directed at the use of NDAs in UK
universities, a sector which has been marketised relatively recently
(McGettigan 2013; Slaughter & Rhoades 2004) and has consequently
increased the resources aimed at enhancing market position through
brand image and reputation management (Cronin 2016). A BBC investigation in 2020 used Freedom of Information (FOI) requests to
reveal that almost a third of UK universities had used NDAs in cases
in which students had made complaints about sexual assault, false advertising of degree courses, inadequate disability support and issues
relating to accommodation (Croxford 2020). Although Universities
UK, a body representing 140 UK universities, reportedly stated that
NDAs should not be used by universities to deal with student griev-
ances, there was evidence of at least 300 NDAs across 45 universities
since 2016 and that £1.3 m had been paid out as part of such confidentiality agreements (Croxford 2020). The use of NDAs in the university
sector can be seen as part of a PR strategy to protect and enhance
individual institutions' 'reputational capital' (Cronin 2016) and ex-
emplifies how the 'soft' tactics of PR reputational enhancement and
positive media coverage interface with the blunt force of the law in
the use of NDAs as a social technology of secrecy and silencing. This
is a dynamic interface which responds to social shifts: the revelations
that some universities use NDAs in relation to cases of sexual assault
and sexual harassment has since come to have a negative impact on
the same reputational capital that universities were aiming to protect with the use of NDAs and they now appear to be shifting their
position. A 2022 UK government press release reports that six university vice-chancellors 'have signed up to a pledge promising not to
use NDAs in dealing with complaints of sexual misconduct, bullying,
and other forms of harassment' and that all universities have been
encouraged to sign the pledge.[8]

While the legally binding status of NDAs may be ambiguous, and those who have instigated the NDA may never actually sue an individual who breaks the terms of that NDA, the force of the NDA resides in its threat. As I explore below in relation to another social technology of secrecy – the DSMA-Notice – the power of such means of concealment is multi-dimensional: they can materially obfuscate or control the flow of information, but they also contribute to the more general secrecy–publicity dynamic that shapes social relations. As illustrated in the case of PR publicity's intersection with the secrecy practices of universities' use of NDAs, that relationship between publicity and secrecy is embedded in a range of social practices and discourses and shifts alongside them.

Previously known as D notices or DA notices, DSMA-Notices are voluntary guidelines relating to the publication or broadcasting of information that may compromise UK national security.[9] Produced by the UK's Defence and Security Media Advisory Committee, the guidelines have no legal force and comprise various 'standing notices' relating to sensitive areas such as military operations and nuclear facilities. The DSMA Committee is 'an independent, advisory body composed of senior civil servants and editors from national and regional newspapers, periodicals, news agencies, television, radio and digital publishers'.[10] The Committee is not subject to the Freedom of Information Act 2000 or the Freedom of Information (Scotland) Act of 2002, but it is 'committed to practising a policy of maximum disclosure of its activities consistent with the effective conduct of its business and the need to ensure that it honours any assurance of confidentiality given to the individuals and organisations with which it deals'.[11]

Although one participant, Rachel Oldroyd, former Managing Editor and CEO of the Bureau of Investigative Journalism, said that she had had some experience of DSMA-Notices when she worked as a journalist for *The Mail on Sunday* newspaper, most journalists in my study had never come across the issue of DSMA-Notices or potential restrictions to what they could publish or broadcast because of the DSMA-Notice system.[12] In an account typical of other journalists in my study, Richard Sambrook, who had worked for 15 years at the BBC as a programme editor, states that D notices were simply not an issue in the everyday work of BBC news:

> I don't think it's some great scheme of national censorship as some people seem to think it is. I can honestly say… in 15 years as a national programme editor, and manager of the… biggest newsroom in the country, I don't think I ever had any D notice issues

come up at all and that was through several wars that Britain was involved in.

An investigative journalist at a national newspaper comments similarly on the limited restrictive impact of DSMA-Notices:

> It has never once been an issue. The only time I come across it is people speculating on the internet that the reason we're not writing about the story they wish we were writing about is because of some vast conspiracy where the government has ordered us not to publish things. If the government went around ordering us not to publish things we would never have published the [x] investigation. You know, I get slightly irritated by it. It tends to end up being just hurled at you as an allegation as to why you're not writing about a subject people would like you to be writing about... I'm completely unaware of [DSMA-Notices] ever having been an issue.
>
> (participant 33)

This journalist notes that censorship and restrictions on media freedom are imagined by the public to be the key driving forces behind journalists' selection of stories to investigate and publish. Public perceptions of this sort follow the logic of conspiracy theories which tend to be characterised by beliefs that everything is connected in hidden but powerful ways, that information is out there if you can only find it and that there are elite groups who control society, and particularly the media, while themselves remaining concealed (see Butter & Knight 2020). As Richard Sambrook suggests, there may be a public perception that governments or elite groups exert tight control over that which circulates in the media sphere and that which is concealed, and that the DSMA-Notice system – if they public were aware of it – would likely be understood as a powerful manifestation of this. But this perception of systematic censorship distracts from the more banal but widespread ways in which secrecy operates, such as the 'culture of secrecy' that may develop in certain organisations.[13]

> Institutional culture has a big role to play.... The BBC was culturally very conservative and still does, to a degree, try to say as little as possible because as soon as it says anything there are, you know, a whole bunch of people who want to have a go at it. So it may to some extent may be justified because it's a sort of controversial institution that whatever it does or doesn't say people will want to attack it. So you know they try to manage that down by

saying as little as possible.... You don't need to be heavy-handed about saying keep something secret if the culture is strong enough that people know that's not what we do around here, we don't talk about that stuff.... I'm sure that's [also] true in government. I'm sure it's true in big commercial companies.

(Richard Sambrook, former BBC editor, participant 35)

If an institutional culture is founded on a conservative approach to the disclosure of information, there is less need for overt censorship or formal controls (Costas & Grey 2016). As Simmel (1906) notes in relation to secret societies, members are socialised into secrecy, embedding a default tendency that militates against disclosure. Further, by focusing on perceived media censorship in the United Kingdom – exemplified in the DSMA-Notice system as a tool of media control – attention is diverted from the common mechanisms through which power is actually wielded (such as the threat and application of legal measures). Such legal processes remain largely obscure to the general public. Such processes may themselves be legally subject to reporting restrictions by super-injunctions, so they do not figure in public perceptions of how secrecy operates. This itself is another form of secret.

In this chapter, I have argued that while NDAs and DSMA-Notices both function as social technologies of secrecy that shape social relations, they do not operate quite as the public may imagine. The legal status of NDAs may be ambiguous (in that they cannot in law prevent people divulging issues that are illegal or dangerous, and cannot prevent whistleblowing in the public interest), but they promote secrecy and effect concealment through threat and the establishment of a culture of secrecy. DSMA-Notices are voluntary codes rather than state censorship and impact little on everyday practices of journalism. Yet they function as social technologies of secrecy in three key ways: they shape practices of concealment in the ways described above; they shape public understandings about secrecy and the media (although in ways not well-aligned with the reality of the situation); they contribute to the secrecy–publicity dynamic as explored in more detail in the next chapter.

Notes

1 However, PR's use of social media can bypass journalists as gatekeepers of public communication. On gatekeeping as a concept, see Vos (2015).
2 Many journalists have also chosen to leave the profession and have become public relations practitioners. Participants in my study talked of better pay, hours, job security, and more chances of career advancement in PR compared to journalism.

3 A UK government department: Department for Environment, Food and Rural Affairs.
4 Data journalists are often paired with 'traditional' journalists to work on a story.
5 At the time of writing, an EU directive has been proposed to target SLAPP suits aimed at journalists. 'And in a move against London – often called the libel capital of Europe – courts in member states would be able to refuse to recognise or enforce judgments in Slapp cases from non-EU countries' (Rankin 2022).
6 https://www.lawsociety.org.uk/public/for-public-visitors/common-legal-issues/workplace-problems/confidentiality-clauses-and-non-disclosure-agreements. Accessed 3/5/22.
7 For example, see: 'NDAs misused in casting – actors and agents warn', https://www.bbc.co.uk/news/entertainment-arts-60072795. Accessed 4/5/22. 'Former Channel 4 News employee 'traumatised' after signing NDA', https://www.theguardian.com/media/2022/feb/10/former-channel-4-news-employee-traumatised-after-signing-nda. Accessed 4/5/22.
8 https://www.gov.uk/government/news/universities-pledge-to-end-use-of-non-disclosure-agreements. Accessed 9/2/22. In 2022, Universities UK (UUK) which represents the sector has recommended that no universities use NDAS in such circumstances https://www.universitiesuk.ac.uk/latest/news/staff-student-sexual-misconduct-be. Accessed 18/7/22.
9 See the UK's Defence and Security Media Advisory Committee (DSMA) web site: https://www.dsma.uk/.
10 https://www.dsma.uk/about/. Accessed 8/2/22.
11 https://www.dsma.uk/about/. Accessed 8/2/22.
12 Leigh (1980) notes the decline of the D notice system in his account of secrecy and journalism in the 1960s and 1970s Britain.
13 The political and ideological orientation of media owners also plays a large role in the selection of issues to report and the framing of that reporting, and media ownership is becoming increasing concentrated in the UK (Media Reform Coalition 2021).

References

Boumans, J. (2018) 'Subsidizing the news? Organizational press releases' influence on news media's agenda and content', *Journalism Studies*, 19(15): 2264–2282.
Bourne, C. (2022) 'Our platformised future', in J. Zylinska (ed) *The Future of Media*, London: Goldsmiths. pp. 86–95.
Butter, M. & P. Knight (eds) (2020) *Routledge Handbook of Conspiracy Theories*. London & New York: Routledge.
Cairncross, F. (2019) *The Cairncross Review: A Sustainable Future for Journalism*. https://assets.publishing.service.gov.uk/government/uploads/system/uploads/attachment_data/file/779882/021919_DCMS_Cairncross_Review_.pdf. Accessed 19/4/22.
Costas, J. & C. Grey (2016) *Secrecy at Work: The Hidden Architecture of Organizational Life*. Stanford: Stanford University Press.

Couldry, N. & A. Hepp (2016) *The Mediated Construction of Reality*, Oxford: Polity Press.

Cronin, A. M. (2018) *Public Relations Capitalism: Promotional Culture, Publics and Commercial Democracy*. Basingstoke: Palgrave.

Cronin, A.M. (2016) 'Reputational capital in "the PR University": public relations and market rationalities', *Journal of Cultural Economy*, 9(4): 396–409.

Croxford, R. (2020) 'Sexual assault claims "gagged" by UK universities', https://www.bbc.co.uk/news/uk-51447615. Accessed 14/2/20.

Curran, J. (2022) 'An end to futility: a modest proposal', in J. Zylinska (ed) *The Future of Media*, London: Goldsmiths. pp. 42–52.

Cushion, S., J. Lewis & R. Callaghan (2017) 'Data journalism, impartiality and statistical claims', *Journalism Practice*, 11(10): 1198–1215.

Davies, N. (2009) *Flat Earth News: An Award-winning Reporter Exposes Falsehood, Distortion and Propaganda in the Global Media*. London: Vintage.

Dean, J. (2002) *Publicity's Secret: How Technoculture Capitalizes on Democracy*. New York: Cornell University Press.

Fletcher, R. & R. K. Nielsen (2018) 'Are people incidentally exposed to news on social media? A comparative analysis', *New Media & Society*, 20(7): 2450–2468.

Forde, S. & J. Johnston (2013) 'The news triumvirate: public relations, wire agencies and online copy', *Journalism Studies*, 14(1): 113–129.

Franklin, B. (2010) 'Sources, credibility and the continuing crisis of UK journalism', in B. Franklin, B. & M. Carlson (eds) *Journalists, Sources, and Credibility: New Perspectives*. London & New York: Routledge. pp. 90–106.

Gandy, O. H. (1982) *Beyond Agenda Setting: Information Subsidies and Public Policy*. New York: Ablex.

Gans, H. J. (2003) *Democracy and the News*. Oxford: Oxford University Press.

Hilson, C. J. (2016) 'Environmental SLAPPs in the UK: threat or opportunity?', *Environmental Politics*, 25(2): 248–267.

Jackson, D. & K. Moloney (2016) 'Inside churnalism: PR, journalism and power relationships in flux', *Journalism Studies*, 17(6): 763–780.

Le Cam, F. & D. Domingo (2015) 'The tyranny of immediacy: gatekeeping practices in French and Spanish online newsrooms', in Vos, T. & F. Heinderyckx (eds) *Gatekeeping in Transition*. London & New York: Routledge. pp. 123–140.

Leigh, D. (2019) *Investigative Journalism*. Cham: Palgrave Macmillan.

Leigh, D. (1980) *The Frontiers of Secrecy: Closed Government in Britain*. London: Junction Books.

Lewis, J., A. Williams & B. Franklin (2008a) 'A compromised fourth estate? UK journalism, public relations and news sources', *Journalism Studies*, 9(1): 1–20.

Lewis, J., A. Williams & B. Franklin (2008b) 'Four rumours and an explanation', *Journalism Practice*, 2(1): 27–45.

Lewis, J., S. Cushion & J. Thomas (2005) 'Immediacy, convenience or engagement? An analysis of 24-hour news channels in the UK', *Journalism Studies*, 6(4): 461–477.

Macnamara, J. (2016) 'The continuing convergence of journalism and PR: new insights for ethical practice from a three-country study of senior practitioners', *Journalism & Mass Communication Quarterly*, 93(1): 118–141.

McChesney, R. W. (2012) 'Farewell to journalism?', *Journalism Studies*, 13(5–6): 682–694.

McGettigan, A. (2013) *The Great University Gamble: Money, Markets and the Future of Higher Education*, London: Pluto Press.

Media Reform Coalition (2021) *Who Owns the UK Media?* https://www.mediareform.org.uk/wp-content/uploads/2021/03/Who-Owns-the-UK-Media_final2.pdf

Moloney, K. & C. McGrath (2020) *Rethinking Public Relations: Persuasion, Democracy and Society* (3rd ed). London: Routledge.

Murphy, D. & L. Moerman (2018) 'SLAPPing accountability out of the public sphere', *Accounting, Auditing & Accountability Journal*, 31(6): 1774–1793.

Pagan, V. (2021) 'The murder of knowledge and the ghosts that remain: non-disclosure agreements and their effects', *Culture and Organization*, 27(4): 302–317.

Phillips, G. (2021) '"The rich don't always fight fair": Guardian lawyers, libel and lawsuits', *The Guardian*, 11th October, https://www.theguardian.com/media/2021/oct/11/lawyers-lawsuits-libel-rich-snowden-windrush-investigations. Accessed 11/10/21.

Phillips, A. (2010) 'Old sources: new bottles. Journalists and their sources online', in N. Fenton (ed) *New Media, Old News: Journalism and Democracy in a Digital Age*. London: Sage. pp. 87–101.

Rankin, J. (2022) 'EU announces plans to protect journalists from vexatious lawsuits', *The Guardian*, 27 April. https://www.theguardian.com/media/2022/apr/27/eu-announces-plans-protect-journalists-vexatious-lawsuits-anti-slapp? Accessed 3/5/22.

Reese, S. D. (2021) *The Crisis of the Institutional Press*. Cambridge, MA: Polity Press.

Schudson, M. (2018) *Why Journalism Still Matters*. Cambridge, MA: Polity Press.

Selva, M. (2020) *Fighting Words: Journalism Under Assault in Central and Eastern Europe*. Reuters Institute for the Study of Journalism. https://reutersinstitute.politics.ox.ac.uk/sites/default/files/2020-01/MSelva-Journalism_Under_Assault_FINAL_0.pdf. Accessed 4/5/22.

Simmel, G. (1906) 'The sociology of secrecy and of secret societies', *American Journal of Sociology*, 11(4): 441–498.

Slaughter, S. & G. Rhoades (2004) *Academic Capitalism and the New Economy: Markets, State, and Higher Education*. Baltimore, MD: The Johns Hopkins University Press.

Van Dijck, J., T. Poell & M. de Waal (2018) *The Platform Society. Public Values in a Connective World*. New York: Oxford University Press.

Vos, T. (2015) 'Revisiting gatekeeping theory during a time of transition', in Vos, T. & F. Heinderyckx (eds) *Gatekeeping in Transition.* London & New York: Routledge. pp. 3–24.

Waisbord, S. & A. Russell (2020) 'News flashpoints: networked journalism and waves of coverage of social problems', *Journalism & Mass Communication Quarterly*, 97(2): 376–392.

Williams, A. & S. Gajevic (2013) 'Selling science?: source struggles, public relations, and UK press coverage of animal–human hybrid embryos', *Journalism Studies*, 14(4): 507–522.

Willig, I. (2022) 'From audiences to data points: the role of media agencies in the platformization of the news media industry', *Media, Culture & Society*, 44(1): 56–71.

5   Revelation and secrecy in PR and news media cultures

This chapter examines revelation in the context of news media, focusing on certain key aspects of journalists' investigative practices and on PR practitioners' use of press releases. Revelation is a specific mode of publicity and an important element of the secrecy–publicity dynamic. As defined by Simmel (1906), publicity centres on the making public of information, actions, interests and so on. Previous chapters have examined how PR attempts to shape such publicity in order to gain positive promotional news coverage for clients or to outweigh negative coverage, and I have explored how journalists' practices of making issues public interface with PR work. In this chapter, I explore how the processes, principles, practices and legislation associated with investigation and revelation interface with practices of secrecy and generally circulating discourses of secrecy. I examine journalists' use of Freedom of Information (FOI) requests, the phenomena of leaks, whistleblowing and 'flying kites' and the role of narrative in giving shape and impact to revelation and information release, including in PR press releases. Using the example of a UK government publication, the Cygnus Report (2017), I analyse how practices of secrecy themselves draw on and fuel practices of investigation and revelation.

FOI requests and secrecy–publicity

In their practices of researching news stories, journalists often operate in conditions of uncertainty – they may sense the existence of a newsworthy issue to pursue without knowing its parameters or potential. As one journalist puts it:

> You have to try and pierce the kind of protective shell around the secret that you think you're going for. I mean, the job itself is intrinsically challenging in the sense that you're trying to find out

DOI: 10.4324/9781003369585-5

something that you don't know yet. So you'll often be pursuing a lead but you don't know the full story or you've just got a sense that something is not right here and... you're having to manoeuvre in the dark.

(participant 33)

One of the key tools used by UK journalists to investigate a story, or to assess the potential of a lead, is the FOI request. While journalists engage in a wide range of practices, their use of FOI requests is of particular interest to this study as it exposes the dynamics of concealment and revelation (secrecy and publicity) and shows how they are nested within a broader news media culture.

In the United Kingdom, public access to certain forms of information is governed by the Freedom of Information Act (FOIA) 2000[1] and the Freedom of Information (Scotland) Act (FOISA) 2002.[2] The FOI legislation has a strong political resonance as, 'it symbolises a popular transfer of sovereignty of power and influence from an elite to the populace' (Worthy 2017: 187), although, as I outline below, journalists are frequently confronted by its limitations as a tool for revelation. Under FOI laws, UK public authorities such as the NHS or the police force are required to publish information about their activities and members of the public are entitled to request information from them.[3] This covers a wide range of recorded information such as documents, emails, photographs, computer files, sound or video recordings, meta-data of computer files and CCTV footage. The Information Commissioner's Office (ICO) provides clarification about the parameters of the legislation, outlining certain exemptions:

> It would cost too much or take too much staff time to deal with the request; the request is vexatious; the request repeats a previous request from the same person.... Some exemptions relate to a particular type of information, for instance, information relating to government policy. Other exemptions are based on the harm that would arise or would be likely arise from disclosure, for example, if disclosure would be likely to prejudice a criminal investigation or prejudice someone's commercial interests.... However, most exemptions are not absolute but require you to apply a public interest test. This means you must consider the public interest arguments before deciding whether to disclose the information. So you may have to disclose information in spite of an exemption, where it is in the public interest to do so.[4]

The efficacy of FOI legislation as an investigative tool is not the focus of my analysis; rather, I aim to understand its role in the wider dynamics of secrecy and publicity in the media sphere.[5]

Journalists in my study commented that they frequently use FOI requests when researching stories (see also Hayes 2009) and that learning how to formulate a FOI request precisely was key to achieving good results.

> Knowing what to ask for is actually really at the core of using it well... when I started had made the mistake of using FOI as a battering ram whereas actually it's a scalpel. If you fire a very broad FOI request off to a government agency... you're going to run up against a cost threshold or an exemption or whatever. Whereas if you use it in a much more targeted way, because you've done some background reading and you know that a particular meeting was held on a certain day and there will probably be bits from that meeting, or that you know a meeting with a minister was arranged by the press office and so you can ask the press office for the correspondence, if it's much more targeted it tends to generate results because at the very least they will have to confirm whether or not the information exists... and then it often just becomes a process of getting it out of them.
>
> (participant 33)

While honing the focus of a FOI request can enhance its chances of success, there are various limitations to the FOI system as it relates to journalists' work. The FOI Act encompasses only UK public bodies and can only capture that which has been recorded and archived. The introduction of the legislation has led some organisations to develop defensive tactics, such as avoiding recording certain information in written form in order to escape the reach of FOI requests (see Chapter 3). Journalists in my study commented that individuals working for public bodies have started using unofficial channels to communicate in ways they hope will be less publicly visible or accessible to FOI requests, such as the private messaging platforms WhatsApp and Signal. In addition, the use of the FOI Act – and transparency measures more generally – is no guarantee of the accuracy of any information that may be released. This may not represent an attempt on the part of organisations to deliberately mislead. Organisations may believe that the information in question is correct, and indeed they may be acting on it within the organisation, yet the information may be inaccurate or incomplete. Organisations may also intentionally frustrate FOI requests. They may release requested information in a deliberately unwieldy form which renders it hard to search and analyse, and they can delay responding to a request: 'many organisations have been digging their heels in and delaying, prevaricating and sometimes don't really answer at all' (participant 20) (see also Hayes 2009). Journalists also commented that some organisations, including government bodies, are strategically unforthcoming about what information may, in fact, exist, or will use legal proceedings to block access to information:

> So as soon as you make a request, if it's something controversial, they will get their lawyers to look at it, and they will not say, 'oh, what does he want to know?', they'll say, 'what exactly does the law require us to do?... what can we get away with?' And that's what happened, [in a particular case] they were blocking me at every point by quibbling about this or that aspect of the law... the Act says that there is a duty on the public body to assist a member of the public in obtaining the information they want, an overriding duty, really. So if I say... 'I want to find out about such and such' and they say 'well, that's too vague, it's too general', they should [actually] be saying to me 'tell me a little bit more about what it is you're after and I'll see if I can find where that stuff might be'. Instead of which they say, 'too general'. So then you come back and say, 'well ok, have you got any documents relating to X?', and they say 'still too general'. 'Ok, well, what about a document about this or about that?', and then they'll say 'oh, well, that document is restricted in some way'.... They should be saying, 'ok, we can't give you that document, but there is information we can give you'. So it's a very obstructive process.
>
> (former newspaper and broadcast journalist, participant 1)

In these ways, journalists' access to official information can be mediated by the narrow parameters of the FOI Act, the various ways that organisations may comply with either the letter or the spirit of the law, and also by organisations' PR practitioners:

> I think, in terms of gathering information, public bodies are easier because you can use the FOI. Corporations are harder because they have no obligation to talk to you or to provide you with information. In terms of dealing with PR... representatives... I often find that companies are actually much better because civil servants again tend to be quite withholding, whereas company PR officers often tend to take the attitude that the [national newspaper's]

investigations team is onto them and the game is up, so you might as well, you know, do damage limitation and put a good spin on it.

(participant 33)

What is notable in journalists' use of FOI requests – and how such practices of revelation interface with PR practices of obfuscation or the release of strategically formulated information – is how it reveals the generative tension that exists between practices of secrecy on the one hand and practices of publicity and revelation on the other. This dynamic tension is evident in the process of investigation: journalists speculate about the existence of further information on the basis of what is already in the public domain, a task akin to fitting jigsaw pieces into the blank spaces left in the puzzle. When working on stories about knife crime and about rape prosecutions, one journalist described how their team calculated the range of data that might be available and how they reverse-engineered the detail and focus of their FOI requests on the basis of this estimate:

Usually [the key thing] is first knowing that something exists. So there was a data set in the public domain and it answers part of your question but it doesn't really go deep enough.... And so it was knowing that something existed that gathered data by homicide using a knife, that was the first step. And then I spoke to people and found out what the data set was, who held it, what other kind of things were in it, and then got the data dictionary questions that they ask in order to make the data set. So having been armed with that, and knowing that it exists, was a really useful way of leveraging to give us the stuff. It's the same with the CPS [Crime Prosecution Service][6] around rape prosecutions and knowing that this database exists, knowing the kinds of things that they can pull out of it was really helpful.

(participant 23)

In effect, the journalist estimated the nature and parameters of the existing but invisible information – the secret – by extrapolating from the visible traces left by the production of the information that was being held, in this case the questions that were used to generate the data set.

This shifting, generative relationship between secrecy and publicity is also evident in journalists' practices of using FOI requests to test out organisations' tender spots or to uncover what types of information organisations may wish to keep secret. As one journalist put it, FOI requests can be a powerful tool even if they do not result in a release of information as, 'they're useful in discovering precisely what they don't want you to know' (Gary Younge, former journalist at *The Guardian* newspaper). Knowing the parameters of what you do not know, and understanding what an organisation may be sensitive about, will provide leads about how to refine subsequent FOI requests in order to leverage the release of certain information and will illuminate the broader significance of that information.

As well as suggesting that something has been concealed and hinting at its form and content, that which is visible in the public realm also stimulates a powerful drive to locate and reveal that which is obscured. This impetus to uncover and make public can be amplified by an organisation's attempts to layer further secrecy measures onto an issue. One journalist gives the example of a new UK body with a remit to engage in high-risk scientific research, The Advanced Research and Invention Agency, which the government has exempted from the FOI Act[7]:

> The government has announced that it's going to put, I think it's ten billion, over however many years into a body that funds high risk, high reward scientific research… the idea being that this is what the Americans did in the Seventies and it created the internet, so we should do the same thing here. It's a perfectly reasonable idea. However, the body is now going to be exempt from the Freedom of Information Act, so I would imagine that the reasoning for this is… because it's going to invest in lots of high risk, high reward projects, lots of high risk projects won't come off and journalists would… file FOI request and find out that, you know, a hundred million pounds has been wasted on trying to create a programme to download rice or something, and we'd write horrible articles about it. But by making it secret from the FOI Act, you come across the same secrecy disease problem that I mentioned before, which is that all you have done is turn every unsuccessful venture into a sort of hidden scandal that's waiting to be uncovered. Exempting the thing from FOI doesn't inoculate the body against public scrutiny, it just tells journalists that they've got something to go at. It's a very bad approach. And I think that's slightly emblematic of this particular government's attitude to secrecy which is, you know, they don't realise how hard it makes the job for them sometimes.
>
> (participant 33)

Simply by exempting it from the FOI Act, the UK government is making this new body a more appealing target for journalists and other parties wishing to expose government practices and expenditure. As Simmel (1906) argues, secrets want to be told; they tug at our attention. As I explore in a later section on narrative, the perception that secrets may exist creates a dynamic in which each revelation encourages a sense that there is yet more to be revealed.

This tension can be exemplified in the case of the UK government's 2017 Cygnus Report.[8] In an annex to a 2020 policy paper, the government describes the 2016 Exercise Cygnus as:

> ... a cross-government exercise to test the UK's response to a serious influenza pandemic that took place over 3 days in October 2016 and involved more than 950 people. The Department of Health and Social Care (DHSC) (known as the Department of Health at the time) and 12 other government departments, as well as NHS Wales, NHS England (NHSE), Public Health England (PHE), local public services, several prisons, and staff from the Scottish, Welsh and Northern Ireland governments took part in the exercise. The aim was to test systems to the extreme, to identify strengths and weaknesses in the UK's response plans, which would then inform improvements in our resilience.[9]

Yet this information, and the Cygnus Report itself, was not made publicly available until 2020. Elements of the report's findings were leaked to *The Telegraph* newspaper (see Nuki & Gardner 2020) and *The Guardian* newspaper later reported more detail, noting difficulties in accessing information from the report: 'In a response to a freedom of information request, the Department of Health claimed that the report needed to be kept secret so as to inform policy development' (Pegg 2020). A journalist describes the dynamics that governmental practices of secrecy set up and then fuelled:

> [The UK government] decided that the report had to be kept completely secret and when the Coronavirus pandemic started somebody breathed a word of this to *The Telegraph* who then wrote an article about how... the government was sitting on this report. That it was too terrifying – that was the quote – to be released to the public, and people were asking for it in parliament or asking questions of government ministers in interviews and they refused to release it. Somebody eventually leaked it to *The Guardian* and [they] just published it. It wasn't remotely terrifying. It was written

in the kind of turgid, bloodless language of civil servants and it found problems, lots of problems, and the question was whether they had been resolved. But by keeping it secret they effectively created vastly more work for themselves and vastly more trouble. Had it been published in 2016: (a) there wouldn't have been an entire media [frenzy] about keeping it secret; (b) somebody might have read it and said, 'well, my organisation needs to prepare because that was a problem in this exercise and, you know, I'm a public health official, so I'm going to fix my processes to improve our provision and be better placed to deal with it'; and c) it would've just saved a load of civil servants' time. A doctor brought a judicial review against the government to try and force them to release the report and all its accompanying documentation and if they'd just bloody published the damn thing back in 2016 none of this would have happened, and, of course, the document is now out there and the sky hasn't fallen in, so why was it being kept secret in the first place?

(participant 33)

By initially keeping the report and its findings secret, the government created a media frenzy centring on the revelation of precisely that which it wished to remain obscured. Each governmental obstruction further spurred journalists to imagine enticing controversies that would make excellent scoops and expanding possibilities for striking news reports. As the journalist above notes, this created a dynamic that generated unnecessary controversy for the government, as well as restricting information that may have proved useful for organisations in preparing for potential pandemics.

The appeal of revelation has another intriguing dimension. There is an intense public interest in the revelation of the power dynamics behind the appearance of news stories, and in particular how vested interests and PR shape the news agenda. As Jim Waterson, Media Editor of *The Guardian* newspaper comments, 'there is an enormous appetite now for stories which basically go "ah ha! And the reason you read that was PR!"'. In his view, the UK public is drawn to stories which expose the behind-the-scenes mechanisms of news generation: how PR often succeeds in influencing the parameters and content of the news agenda; the extent of lobbying and its impact and how PR can set up fake grassroots support for certain controversial issues (see the discussion of 'astroturfing' in Chapter 3). This element of the secrecy–publicity dynamic references what Foucault (1990: 73) describes as 'the strategies of power' that are immanent in 'the will to knowledge'. Foucault argues that we need to appreciate the appeal of both truth-seeking and sharing that truth: 'the pleasure of knowing that truth, of discovering and exposing it, the fascination of seeing it and telling it, of captivating and capturing others by it, of confiding it in secret, of luring it out in the open' (Foucault 1990: 71). For Foucault, this drive for truth as a core element of today's societies is linked to the establishment of cultures of confession as a form of governmentality and a general post-Enlightenment shift towards visibility as a mode of power relations (Foucault 1980).

In news cultures, the appeal of revelation is long-established and journalism has fed on, and has in turn fed, public fascination for uncovering secrets and hidden power plays (for example, see Lashmar 2020; Norton-Taylor 2020). But the particular character of revelation's appeal can shift in relation to social and cultural developments. As Jim Waterson notes,

> There's a much greater awareness among the public for bullshit and the moment that you call something out for being inauthentic, then you lose the case in a way you didn't used to. Because 15 years ago, which newspaper was really going to bother pointing it out? But now someone on Twitter will do a thread [saying] 'there's [apparently] a grassroots uprising for X but actually everyone is against it.'
>
> (Jim Waterson, Media Editor of *The Guardian* newspaper, participant 2)

The extent to which the public is genuinely fascinated by details of lobbying or PR practices of obfuscation is unclear, but there is certainly evidence of a strong public interest in revelation relating to celebrities (Marshall 2014) and exposés of the alleged 'inauthenticity' of the words or actions of individuals in the public eye (see Banet-Weiser 2012). In general terms, then, social media can circulate and amplify both 'the will to knowledge' and 'the fascination of seeing it and telling it' (Foucault 1990: 73, 71) in new and more intense ways, and can magnify the appeal of uncovering hidden power relations. This public fascination for revelation – exposing how news can be secretly shaped by vested interests or exposés relating to celebrities – is part of the dynamics of secrecy–publicity that Simmel (1906) describes. It adds hurdles to PR's task of securing positive news coverage and PR's goal of generating influence without exposing its work behind the scenes.

It is important to recognise that the specificities of the social, political and economic context play a key role in shaping the dynamic between secrecy practices and the revelation of information in the public domain. The political context can strongly influence what one journalist calls the 'market for secrets':

> I do remember, just as a kind of indication of how things can shift with politics, not long after the Macpherson report,[10] I following up on the story of a black man who had been working as a security guard and he was arrested for breaking into the place that he was protecting. But he wasn't breaking into it, he was protecting it. And I called the Met [the Metropolitan Police], and said, 'look what's this about?' And I told them the bare bones of the story and then I called them at maybe 2pm and then they called me back at 4pm and they said 'look, we're trying to follow this up' and… 'we're going to ask you if you could hold off publishing it given the sensitivities and blah blah'. No, because I've given you enough time. That was not secrecy exactly, but it was a request not to publish. And the reason I think that's intriguing is because I think five years before or five years later they wouldn't have cared… [my story] just landed in that [politically sensitive moment about race and policing] which is my point about the market for secrets and what needs to be a secret at any given time depends on who they think is going to care one way or the other.
>
> (Gary Younge, former journalist at *The Guardian*, participant 22)

Making a similar point about the specific value of, and sensitivities about, certain information a few months into the Covid-19 pandemic, the same journalist commented, 'If I called a hospital three months ago and said, "how many facemasks have you got?", they'd probably just tell me. They [would have] thought it was weird, but they would tell me. If I called them now, well, there's a market for that kind of information and they would be more secretive about it' (Gary Younge, participant 22). More broadly, the way in which the UK FOI system is functioning – as a tool of publicity to reveal that which is in the realm of secrets – can be seen as a litmus test for a particular political context. One journalist comments on how FOI requests to government are rebuted more often than in the past and links this to the particular political proclivities and priorities of the UK government (in 2021): 'FOI is… an indicator of how governments… treat transparency and how accountable they should be. And I don't think it's working as well as it used to' (participant 23). Having noted the general attitude of a specific government to issues of openness, the journalist goes on to describe the impact of particular socio-political circumstances on practices of secrecy:

> So with Covid the government response to journalists has been very hostile and I think that that is indicative of a culture where transparency is not encouraged anymore, because they're not engaging with journalists in the traditional forms whereby journalists writing a story will send in some questions and the government will either send them back... a quote or something like background or give them a steer on the facts.... They're not doing that anymore.... They're not responding to journalists' requests anymore... or they're only then responding in the public domain in a defensive manner, trying to discredit the journalism.
>
> (journalist at a national newspaper, participant 23)

The journalist notes that this lack of governmental engagement with journalists' queries may be partly due to the intense workload created by the Covid-19 pandemic, but they remain critical about governmental practices: 'it certainly doesn't give you faith that transparency is encouraged within government with journalists at the moment' (participant 23). The increased volume of data publicly available in the United Kingdom may also have shaped the current government's cautious approach to transparency. As Rachel Oldroyd, former Managing Editor and CEO of the Bureau of Investigative Journalism, comments, 'government and society have become more aware of what information they are making available. The information they don't want to make available, they are... ring-fencing and keeping tight' (participant 36), and there is evidence that many journalists are becoming concerned about the undermining of FOI laws due to lack of resources and government obstruction (Dalton 2021; Pegg 2022).

Running in parallel with organisations' and government responses to FOI requests are practices of leaking, whistleblowing and 'flying kites'. These are specific forms of 'truth-telling' but draw on the same dynamic tension that exists in secrecy–publicity.

Leaks, whistleblowing and flying kites

Journalists' practices of revelation are supported not only by FOI requests but by leaks and whistleblowing. Whistleblowing is the practice of revealing information about activities or intended actions, often within a corporation or government, that are illegal, unsafe or socially detrimental (Bazzichelli 2021; Kenny 2019).[11] Leaks are similar in that they are unauthorised releases of information (generally to the media), but they may not be motivated by the public good (see Jones 2006; Palmer 2000). Like FOI requests, such practices are situated within the broad dynamics of secrecy–publicity and while they have many common elements, they also have specific characteristics. 'Off-the-record' briefings – and the use of unnamed sources (see Carlson 2010) – can also be seen as forms of revelation in parallel to the phenomena of leaking or whistleblowing, and are common means by which information from unnamed sources can circulate in the media without making those sources vulnerable to legal or organisational repercussions both in journalism (Dindler 2015; Malling 2021) and in PR (Dimitrov 2020).

There has been an intensified academic interest in whistleblowing and leaking following high profile cases such as Wikileaks which bring into sharp focus issues of media access to information, the production of 'truth', media ethics and the manipulation of access to information by powerful elites (see Brevini et al. 2013; Munro 2017). In parallel, there is a marked journalistic interest in reporting issues relating to whistleblowing as a practice and to individual whistleblowers (Wahl-Jorgensen & Hunt 2012). Whistleblowing and leaking, and the public narratives that circulate about them, are founded on practices of both secrecy and revelation and feed a sense that secrets abound and await discovery. In the context of my study, both journalists and PR practitioners discussed leaking and whistleblowing as potential modes of revelation. As one PR practitioner comments, organisations are potentially very 'leaky', 'if you've got 1,000 people in your office, you've got 1,000 potential weak points where anything could slip out… you'd have to train reception especially 'cos they're a weak point when it comes to, you know, phone calls from journalists' (participant 10). As one journalist describes:

> … someone says, 'you didn't hear this from me but, this happened and I'd be grateful if you'd keep my name out of it' and there's always quite a lot of important conversations that take place off-the-record, where people will give you guidance…. In the run up to the Iraq war when I was in America we got very good briefings from… the British representatives in the UN, but most of it was off-the-record. And then there'd be a negotiation about [labelling the source of the information], is that a senior British source or is that this, that or the other?
>
> (Gary Younge, former journalist, participant 22)

Journalists in my study commented that they frequently got 'tip offs' and that news outlets now have sections of their web site which openly invite individuals to contact journalists with sensitive information they wish to reveal. For example, *The Guardian* newspaper asks readers to 'Share stories with us securely and confidentially' through its 'Secure-Drop' service which encrypts the contents of emails and allows the secure sharing of files. From a journalist's point of view, today's range of digital technologies and secure platforms offer ever-expanding possibilities for individuals to direct them towards potential stories and for whistleblowers to leak information more easily, although it can be hard to protect the sources (see Danbury & Townend 2019):

> Everyone has a mobile phone with a camera on it. I have Signal and WhatsApp [private messaging platforms]. Someone can send me something that they've taken a photo of – a computer screen – and send it to me in fairly good confidence without worrying too much about what's going on.... Basically, everything is electronic and it's very easy to make a copy of something electronic. You don't have to hope that they can sneak out the Pentagon papers and get it photocopied overnight. You just basically have to hope that someone's got it on a memory stick and can send it to you.
>
> (Jim Waterson, *The Guardian*'s Media Editor, participant 2)

Such technological affordances, Waterson goes on to note, mean that there now exists a culture of leaks and informal, off-the-record briefings:

> There's a massive shift away from public and semi-public messaging to highly encrypted private messaging and so you end up with this bizarre situation [in which] rather than a constant low level of leaks and briefings, you tend to... have stuff stay silent within a WhatsApp group and then the entire WhatsApp group will be leaked to the media.... It sort of bubbles up and then explodes because leaks act as a regulator on bad systems by... correcting for behaviour that isn't being corrected within an organisation.

Journalists commented that the use of private messaging platforms such as WhatsApp or Signal by government officials means that their communications remain below the radar and are not readily accessible for FOI requests or other mechanisms that may ensure transparency. This leads to a problematic lack of accountability, as many journalists commented. The affordances of digital technologies mean that it is harder than ever to ring-fence and control information (Couldry &

Hepp 2016). This, in turn, drives the introduction of new practices oriented towards secrecy, thus fuelling the shifting dynamics that exist between secrecy and publicity. As well as avoiding the recording of sensitive information in written form, the awareness of digital technologies' capacities makes individuals and organisations cautious about putting information online and about recording information in various digital formats. As the journalist Roy Greenslade comments, 'The truth is that if institutions wish to keep secrets, they are going to not put anything online, because everything online is available to us. I was at an [Julian] Assange meeting the other day and... before we even spoke, we all had to turn our mobiles off and they were collected in a different room' (participant 20).

Leaks and whistleblowing can, therefore, form a key source of information for journalists. But if a society were fully transparent, they would likely be redundant. Martin Shipton, a very experienced journalist based in Wales, comments:

> I think that there is sometimes an [incorrect] belief that it's easy [for journalists] to get hold of information, but when it comes to the crunch, for the really juicy pieces of information which are going to discredit a government or a company, you have to rely on whistleblowers, partly because ... the Freedom of Information Act only applies to the public sector, but also because... [of] the exemptions that exist and the public interest test which... can make it possible for an organisation that doesn't want particular a particular piece of information to be released, not to be released. So I think [government bodies and other public institutions] are quite tuned up in this respect and I think they know exactly what they're doing.... These days, on a very regular basis, we read of stories where a leaked report [for example] shows that Liz Truss [a government minister]... is actively planning to reduce food standards in order to get a free trade agreement with the United States. I mean, that's come out because somebody's leaked it. It's not because she's made an announcement. So I think while there is this superficial view [that society is more transparent], which is supported by public bodies – if you look at their websites they'll say, 'we're very open, we're very transparent, make Freedom of Information requests and you'll get the information' – the reality is that if there's something which they really don't want you to know, they will succeed in keeping it from you unless there's somebody within the organisation who's prepared to leak it.
>
> (Martin Shipton, journalist, participant 3)

Alongside these unofficial leaks which may cause embarrassment or difficulties for organisations, government or other bodies can engage in practices of planned leaks known as 'flying kites'. Such practices involve a strategic, anonymous leak of information (often by government) designed to test public opinion on an issue – flying a kite to gauge the direction the wind is blowing (Davis 2009). They are structured such that there is 'plausible deniability' built in: should public opinion appear unfavourable to the leaked information or proposed policy, government can deny that it is true or was ever a proposed government policy. If public opinion appears favourable to it, government can then claim it and develop it. A PR practitioner in my study described the current government's practice, which follows a standard logic of flying kites: 'they leak a story into a friendly outlet like *The Daily Mail* [right-wing UK national newspaper]... don't make a proper announcement... and let's just see how it goes down. You know, what do our... core voters say about it in *The Daily Mail*? And then... maybe we'll announce it, or maybe not. Maybe we just pretend we were never going to do that anyway' (participant 31).

Although they operate in different ways, practices associated with FOI requests, leaks and whistleblowing are all part of the dynamics of revelation which are themselves situated in a shifting tension with practices of secrecy. Such revelations translocate information from the realm of secrecy to the realm of publicity and, in doing so, transform the ontological status of such information from that of *secret held by the few* to that of *knowledge shared by many*, a practice that Simmel (1906) argues creates social groups, social relationships and power dynamics. As social technologies of publicity and revelation, the FOI system, leaks and whistleblowing operate in nuanced ways that intersect with practices of secrecy and obfuscation. Alongside what Foucault (1990: 71) considers the pleasures of truth-seeking and truth-telling – 'the pleasure of knowing that truth... of captivating and capturing others by it, of confiding it in secret, of luring it out in the open' – exist practices of secrecy that pull with compelling force in the other direction. Foucault (2007) notes that the modern state maintains the right to keep secrets while at the same time requiring its citizens to expose themselves to intense state surveillance through various modes of governmentality. Foucault (2007: 275) argues that we require not only a general analysis of practices of governmentality – which includes various forms of rendering individuals, groups and social connections visible – but also an analysis of secrecy that includes, 'a precise codification of what can be and what must not be published'. The practices of FOI, leaks and whistleblowing are some of the key social technologies of secrecy–publicity that are set within, and manage, today's (news) media sphere. FOI requests, leaks and whistleblowing also share a relationship to narrative and narrative structuring, and narratives themselves can act as means of governmentality.

Narrative as a social technology of secrecy–publicity

Creating stories through narratives is a core element of both journalism and PR. Importantly, stories and narrative are not synonymous: "'story' consists of all the events which are to be depicted.... "Narrative" is the showing or the telling of these events and the mode selected for that to take place' (Cobley 2001: 5–6). Journalists must shape information into recognisable stories to act as units of news reporting – short news reports, op-ed pieces, feature articles, long form journalism, investigative exposés and so on – tailoring that information to specific audiences, formats and platforms through narrative practices while ensuring that it is appealing to the reader and clearly articulated (see Vos 2018). Journalists also use other forms of narrative when they pitch stories to editors, as well as in ancillary aspects of their role, such as writing social media posts or blog pieces. A core task of media relations PR is the creation of narratives for public consumption, or 'changing the narrative' of existing media visibility, to emphasise the positive aspects of clients while downplaying any negatives (Edwards 2018; Moloney & McGrath 2020). While there are many differences in aims and execution, the storying or narrative-making practices in both journalism and PR share the context in which they operate: they are interest-driven forms of communication that are shaped by the technological and formal characteristics of the media sphere and are situated within a market-driven media context which requires the capture of audiences or readership. Skilfully conceived and constructed narrative forms will aide in that capture.

But journalism and PR share another relationship to story-making and narrative. The creation of stories, in their various narrative forms, shapes people's experience of the secrecy–publicity dynamic, while the secrecy–publicity dynamic as a socially embedded structuring force acts to shape narrative form in stories. As outlined in my previous discussion of the various news media and PR techniques of secrecy and publicity, a key element of the dynamic involves establishing expectations that secrets exist and that they may be subject to revelation. As Simmel argues, this is a key driver of secrecy practices: 'Secrecy involves a tension which, at the moment of revelation, finds its release' (Simmel 1906: 465). Creating frameworks for that tension and

expectation through narrative form is a powerful technique: people
are familiar with various forms of stories, story-making and narrative, for instance, in oral story-telling, songs, novels, film, television,
biography and autobiography. Roland Barthes (1983: 251) famously
remarked that, 'narrative is present in every age, in every place, in
every society; it begins with the very history of mankind and there
nowhere is nor has been a people without narrative'. Anthropology
has explored how story-making and story-telling is a foundational
element of all societies, and as Lévi-Strauss' (1978) account of myth
demonstrates, stories can function to actively create and maintain social relations and structure societal formations. The social sciences
more generally have explored story-making and narrative both as
research method and as socially constitutive force, examining what
Plummer (2019) calls 'narrative power' and the ways it acts to make
and remake social relations. The most nuanced accounts of story-
making and narrative are located, unsurprisingly, in the field of literary studies. As I outlined in Chapter 2, such analyses provide subtle
and compelling accounts of secrecy and literary forms, revealing how
narrative structuring is central to the mechanisms of both secrecy
and revelation (e.g. Horn 2013; Melley 2012). Such literary studies are
detailed in their exploration of the range of narrative forms and are
sensitive to the power of narrative to shape understanding. Most no-
tably, Paul Ricoeur (1981) explores how narrative operates through
temporal sequencing that sets up expectations for the reader who is,
in turn, active in interpretively connecting events through the antici-
pation of the conclusion.

My interest in narrative does not involve an exploration of literary
accounts of story-making and narrative (see Cobley 2001; Eagleton
1986), or a more general analysis of narrative as a world-making tool
(see Haraway 2019). Instead, my interest is focused more narrowly on
how story-making and narrative forms interface with the secrecy–
publicity dynamic in the context of the media sphere and news culture
in particular. As a framework that explores how language and practice
are both socially embedded and socially generative, Foucault's work
on discourse is sensitive to power relations and social change in ways
which are helpful for this study. I understand narrative as the device
oriented to the showing and telling of selected events or issues and the
mode in which they are told, whereas discourse is the broader framework of intelligibility that acts to bring certain realities into being.
Foucault describes how discourse is not 'a mere intersection of things
and words: an obscure web of things, and a manifest, visible, coloured
chain of words... discourse is not a slender surface of contact, or

confrontation, between a reality and a language (*langue*), the intrication of a lexicon and an experience...' (Foucault 2001: 48). He argues that we should not treat 'discourses as groups of signs (signifying elements referring to contents or representations) but as practices that systematically form the objects of which they speak' (Foucault 2001: 49). Foucault maintains that discourses are productive and they are interwoven with power relations. Nowhere is this more evident than in a society's 'regime of truth':

> Each society has its regime of truth, its 'general politics' of truth: that is, the types of discourse which it accepts and makes function as true; the mechanisms and instances which enable one to distinguish true and false statements, the means by which each is sanctioned; the techniques and procedures accorded value in the acquisition of truth; the status of those who are charged with saying what counts as true.... 'Truth' is to be understood as a system of ordered procedures for the production, regulation, distribution, circulation, and operation of statements. 'Truth' is linked in a circular relation with systems of power which produce and sustain it, and to effects of power which it induces and which extends it. A 'regime' of truth. This regime is not merely ideological or superstructural; it was a condition of the formation and development of capitalism.
>
> (Foucault 1991: 73–74)

Narratives and, of course, journalism are embedded in, draw on and act upon discourses of truth. Much has been written about journalists' textual practices in the creation of news stories in newspapers, online news sites and broadcast contexts (e.g. Allan 2010; Palmer 2000; Vos 2018), but my interest in journalism lies in its practices that uncover and present what constitutes 'news' for any given outlet and how they are shaped by, and exert influence on, the secrecy–publicity dynamic. My focus also encompasses the relationship between PR and journalism which shifts over time. Alongside the expansion of the UK PR industry as described in Chapter 2, journalists and PR practitioners in my study told of a growth in general practices of 'narrative management', often directed by PR. Former BBC editor Richard Sambrook describes processes of narrative management in which, 'you have teams of communication specialists trying to shape and fashion what the narrative is around an organisation or an issue to their own advantage' (participant 35). This is a well-established communications technique, as I have explored in Chapter 3, but which today may have more traction in news cultures as a result of the resourcing crisis in journalism. As Richard Sambrook suggests, 'this notion of managing the narrative about you or your issue, or whatever it is, has now become huge and... therefore the PR aspects of that have grown significantly at a time when journalism is struggling in terms of resources and funding and workload in order to be able to match it'. There is a perception among journalists in my study that their ability to counter the narratives created by PR is an important check and balance to the powerful, well-resourced and interest-driven communications regime generated by the PR industry and its clients.

A core medium of PR is the press release. Although there have been discussions within the PR industry about its relevance today, there is evidence that the press release is still a widely used and efficient tool. It can be understood in narrative terms as 'an episodic autobiographical narrative genre, by which the organization seeks to establish and negotiate its identity with regard to a generalized external public' (Gilpin 2008: 10). The press release is a convenient format in which to communicate with journalists, as a PR practitioner describes, 'loads of people say, oh, the press release is dead, but if you do ever speak to a journalist and say I've got this story, they always say, "can you send me a press release?" So you still need to [produce press releases]' (participant 5). The press release can serve an important function for both journalists and editors:

> The advantage to reporters and editors using this material is its low cost (crucial to the subsidy notion of information subsidies), ease of access, the speed with which it can be republished, and the fact it may be perceived as being easy to process by non-expert journalists. Furthermore, its direct association with a third party may be interpreted as a low risk for a news organisation in terms of verified content and avoiding defamatory or inaccurate information.
>
> (Wheatley 2020: 286)

Some PR practitioners, however, have started referring to press releases as 'news releases' or 'media releases' to dissociate them from the negative image of PR-produced interest-driven copy and to encourage journalists to use their content. There is also evidence that press releases form the content of a significant proportion of news stories, especially in the least well-resourced sectors of journalism which are under intense pressure to produce a large number of news stories in a very short time (Forde & Johnston 2013; Gandy 1982; Jackson & Moloney 2016; Lewis et al. 2008a, 2008b; Macnamara 2016; McChesney 2012; Phillips 2010). The press release produces what is known in the industry as 'oven-ready copy' (journalist Roy Greenslade, participant 20): text which could be used by a journalist in a news story with little or no rewriting. As Francis Ingham, Director General of the Public Relations and Communications Association (PRCA) notes, 'my local paper in Hampshire recently ran a story that had the word "ends" at the end of the story, so they had literally copied and pasted, including ends'[12] (participant 15). In effect, the narrative format of the press release helps PR practitioners communicate a story to journalists in a compelling and convincing manner: 'you need to be able to pitch ideas to them at the right time and in the right way' (Phil Morgan, Deputy CEO of the Chartered Institute of Public Relations, participant 14).

Press releases usually have a very formulaic structure, which is particularly evident at times of crisis for the client, for instance, following a scandal or negative media coverage. Before an investigative news report is published, organisations or individuals will be given an opportunity to respond with a statement, produced by the PR/communications team, which may be included in the news item. This form of 'crisis communication' is aimed at addressing and repairing any reputational damage to the client (Sellnow & Seeger 2013). A journalist neatly describes the typical narrative structure of such press releases:

> There's a certain grammar to these statements.... The first paragraph of that statement will read something to the effect of, 'our company is blah blah blah and has blah blah blah values and we don't stand for anything that's bad and we're a staunch supporter of things that are good'. The second paragraph will read... 'in the process of getting to where we are now, certain historic practices took place that are no longer considered acceptable in the company today'.... There will often be a certain kind of routine to the way that [criticisms or critical news coverage] are fended off and very often the line is that this is something that took place in the past. [There will] be a studied use of the present tense, and with a view to being able to illustrate that whilst this did happen, it doesn't reflect the company anymore.
>
> (participant 33)

Press releases can be framed by PR practitioners as 'counter-narratives' – means of responding to negative mainstream media reporting or critical discussion about their clients on social media. A PR practitioner comments on how PR can struggle to respond to the intensity and breadth of negative commentary on social media:

> Because of the way social media works... it's very linear, so it's black or white, it's good or bad.... So people see things in a very, very stark way in lots of respects.... Where's the counter narrative? Where's the discussion around the positives of what [the client organisation or individual] brought, about the amazing pieces of work that people are doing, about how things happen because of the way the communication and PR world functions. That for me is the problem because we don't get that out in the same way that the counter narrative gets out, the narrative of the negative gets out there.
>
> (participant 30)

Although it may be hard to shape narratives circulating on social media, the press release has considerable traction in news media cultures because it addresses PR practitioners' need to pitch content to journalists in a way that captures their attention; it resources journalists' need for an ever-increasing volume of content while presenting it in a familiar and convenient narrative format that can easily be adapted for use in a news story. As one PR practitioner put it:

> The press release is not dead... ultimately we're telling stories to journalists and our job is to make it as easy as possible for them. The press release still feels to me like the best format we've come up with for getting the story out there to a broader audience. And... it has a structure that journalists understand, PRs understand. It tends to follow a flow, it includes commentary, it includes information. It's just an easy way to digest information.
>
> (participant 12)

This narrative formula taps into the broader, socially embedded understanding of stories as having one of a range of recognisable narrative shapes and modes of revelation and denouement. In effect, the classic PR press release taps into the dynamic tension of the secrecy–publicity relationship. It posits that there is a story to be told, and thus revelations to be made, while offering the format that the narrative could take. In effect, PR press releases and journalists' stories are situated within, and derive their impetus and influence from, the dynamics of secrecy (that which is hidden but can potentially be uncovered) and publicity (that which is in general circulation, that which has been revealed, that which can be apprehended through practices of narration). Although powerful means of orienting communication, PR-generated narratives can backfire, as Burt (2012) describes in relation to the infamous rebranding exercise of the company BP as 'Beyond Petroleum'. This move was widely criticised as 'greenwashing' and stimulated journalists to probe the company's activities.

> Any narrative that promises more than it delivers creates an obvious reputation risk when things go wrong. And it is often the PR function – the in-house team and their outside advisors – that carries the can when a narrative proves illusionary such as BP's much derided 'Beyond Petroleum'. It is the PR team that has to explain to a sceptical media why a narrative was developed in the first place, while avoiding any disclosure of the costs involved and playing down criticism of management. 'Beyond Petroleum' was a classic case of a broken narrative. It demonstrated that a company should only extol such virtues when it has the financial track record, the product pipeline and potential growth opportunities to justify that sort of storyline. Even in the rare cases where such claims are justified, the benefits of a narrative can be undermined by weak or woolly language.
>
> (Burt 2012: 188)

The circulation of a PR press release also functions as a form of meta-commentary: quite apart from the specific content of any one press release, the very act of releasing comment to the media sphere communicates in important ways. PR practitioners noted that when their client is affected by a crisis or scandal, they advise that a response in the form of a press release should be created and circulated (ensuring that the narrative does not include an apology as this may suggest acceptance of liability and leave the client open to legal action). PR practitioners warn clients against 'no commenting' an issue as this may give the appearance of something to hide. The press release should follow the standard 'accept and regret' strategy using the well-established format described above. This illustrates the general point made throughout my analysis that media relations PR operates as a form of visibility management that attempts to manipulate negative perceptions. But it also illustrates the importance of being seen by the public and a client's other audiences (such as regulators), to be active in responding, actively engaging in narrating a story about the issue in question, and active in taking part in discussions in the media sphere. PR practitioners promote the view that publics today *expect* organisations and individuals to be consistently involved in public narrations, whether through social media accounts, advertising and marketing campaigns or contributions in mainstream media sources. The forms of revelation discussed in this chapter tap into and reshape the tension that exists between secrecy and publicity and contribute to the formation of the shadow world of the media sphere described in previous chapters. This shadow world is manifested in pockets of secrecy and is created in the interface between legislation, regulation, technologies' affordances, 'regimes of truth', and norms and practices in media industries and in wider society. These pockets of secrecy are temporary configurations that shift over time in response to wider social, political and economic change. They interface with publicity in ways which generate new configurations: journalists' practices of investigation and revelation, and PR practitioners' shaping of particular forms of disclosure through press releases, both prompt shifts in the tactics of secrecy that are deployed (such as avoiding recording discussions in writing). As I discuss in the final chapter, the narratives produced by PR and journalism are themselves located within, and act upon, broader societal meta-narratives about truth, influence, rights to access information in the public realm (including as a proxy for other democratic rights) and capitalism as a system of distribution of resources.

Notes

1 https://www.legislation.gov.uk/ukpga/2000/36/contents.
2 https://www.legislation.gov.uk/asp/2002/13/contents.
3 Parties who have had FOI requests refused can appeal to the Information Commissioner's Office: 'The UK's independent authority set up to uphold information rights in the public interest, promoting openness by public bodies and data privacy for individuals'. https://ico.org.uk/.
4 https://ico.org.uk/for-organisations/guide-to-freedom-of-information/refusing-a-request/. Accessed 17/2/22.
5 FOI requests have considerable potential for academic research (see Walby & Luscombe 2020).
6 https://www.cps.gov.uk/. 'The Crown Prosecution Service (CPS) prosecutes criminal cases that have been investigated by the police and other investigative organisations in England and Wales. The CPS is independent, and we make our decisions independently of the police and government'.
7 See https://www.gov.uk/government/news/bill-introduced-to-create-high-risk-high-reward-research-agency-aria and https://www.legislation.gov.uk/ukpga/2022/4/contents/enacted.
8 I submitted my own FOI request to the UK government's Department of Health and Social Care asking, 'How many Freedom of Information requests have been made relating to the Cygnus Exercise of 2016 and the

Cygnus report?'. The response illustrates the FOI system's limitations for providing precise information:

> I can confirm that we have conducted a search of the DHSC correspondence database (on which Freedom of Information (FOI) requests are held), using the keyword "Cygnus", and we have identified 41 relevant FOI requests.... Please note, conducting the search using the keyword "Cygnus" would have excluded any FOI requests that may have related to the Exercise, but that did not mention its name specifically. Please also note that whilst we have assessed that 41 FOI requests contain the keyword "Cygnus", they are not necessarily requesting a copy of the Cygnus Report. Requests may have mentioned "Cygnus" as background for other queries, or may have requested a copy of the report after it was published.

9 https://www.gov.uk/government/publications/uk-pandemic-preparedness/annex-a-about-exercise-cygnus. Accessed 22/9/21. The full Cygnus report is available here: https://assets.publishing.service.gov.uk/government/uploads/system/uploads/attachment_data/file/927770/exercise-cygnus-report.pdf. Accessed 16/2/22.
10 The 1999 Macpherson report was the outcome of a government-commissioned inquiry into the racially-motivated murder of Stephen Lawrence and the subsequent police investigation. It found evidence of institutional racism in London's Metropolitan police.
11 In the UK, the practice of whistleblowing is protected under the Public Interest Disclosure Act (1998) https://www.legislation.gov.uk/ukpga/1998/23/contents.
12 The final section of a press release will typically be signalled by placing the word 'ends' in bold or capital letters.

References

Allan, S. (2010) *News Culture*. Maidenhead: Open University Press.
Banet-Weiser, S. (2012) *Authentic™: The Politics of Ambivalence in a Brand Culture*. New York & London: New York University Press.
Barthes, R. (1983) 'Introduction to the structural analysis of narratives', in *Barthes: Selected Writings*. London: Fontana/Collins. pp. 251–295.
Bazzichelli, T. (ed) (2021) *Whistleblowing for Change: Exposing Systems of Power and Injustice*. Bielefeld: transcript Verlag.
Brevini, B., A. Hintz & P. Mccurdy (eds) (2013) *Beyond WikiLeaks: Implications for the Future of Communications, Journalism and Society*, London: Palgrave Macmillan.
Burt, T. (2012) *Dark Art: The Changing Face of Public Relations*. London: Elliott & Thompson.
Carlson, M. (2010) 'Whither anonymity? Journalism and unnamed sources in a changing media environment', in B. Franklin & M. Carlson (eds) *Journalists, Sources, and Credibility: New Perspectives*. London & New York: Routledge. pp. 37–48.
Cobley, P. (2001) *Narrative*. London: Routledge.

Couldry, N. & A. Hepp (2016) *The Mediated Construction of Reality*. Oxford: Polity Press.

Dalton, J. (2021) 'Battle under way over ministers' attempts to silence journalists', *The Independent*, 4 November.

Danbury, R. & J. Townend (2019) 'Can you keep a secret? Legal and technological obstacles to protecting journalistic sources', in S. Price (ed) *Journalism, Power and Investigation: Global and Activist Perspectives*. London & New York: Routledge. pp. 95–111.

Davis, A. (2009) 'Journalist–source relations, mediated reflexivity and the politics of politics', *Journalism Studies*, 10(2): 204–219.

Dimitrov, R. (2020) 'Communicating off the record', *Public Relations Inquiry*, 9(1): 81–102.

Dindler, C. (2015) 'Negotiating political news: the two phases of off-the-record interaction', *Journalism*, 16(8): 1124–1140.

Eagleton, T. (1986) *Literary Theory*. Oxford: Blackwell.

Edwards, L. (2018) *Understanding Public Relations: Theory, Culture and Society*. London: Sage.

Forde, S. & J. Johnston (2013) 'The news triumvirate: public relations, wire agencies and online copy', *Journalism Studies*, 14(1): 113–129.

Foucault, M. (2007) *Security, Territory, Population: Lectures at the College de France, 1977–78*, Arnold I. Davidson (ed). Basingstoke: Palgrave Macmillan.

Foucault, M. (2001) *The Archaeology of Knowledge*, trans. A. M. Sheridan Smith. London: Routledge.

Foucault, M. (1991) 'Truth and power', in P. Rabinow (ed) *The Foucault Reader*. London: Penguin, pp. 51–75.

Foucault, M. (1990) *The History of Sexuality, Volume 1*, trans. Robert Hurley. London: Penguin.

Foucault, M. (1980) *Power/knowledge: Selected interviews and other writings, 1972–1977*. Colin Gordon (ed). New York: Pantheon Books.

Gandy, O. H. (1982) *Beyond Agenda Setting: Information Subsidies and Public Policy*. New York: Ablex.

Gilpin, D. R. (2008) 'Narrating the organizational self: Reframing the role of the news release', *Public Relations Review*, 34(1): 9–18.

Haraway, D. (2019) 'It matters what stories tell stories; it matters whose stories tell stories', *a/b: Auto/Biography Studies*, 34(3): 565–575.

Hayes, J. (2009) 'A shock to the system: journalism, government and the freedom of Information Act 2000', *Reuters institute for the Study of Journalism*. https://reutersinstitute.politics.ox.ac.uk/sites/default/files/2017-11/A%20Shock%20to%20the%20System.pdf. Accessed 6/5/22.

Horn, E. (2013) *The Secret War: Treason, Espionage, and Modern Fiction*, trans. Geoffrey Winthrop-Young. Evanston, IL: Northwestern University Press.

Jackson, D. & K. Moloney (2016) 'Inside churnalism: PR, journalism and power relationships in flux', *Journalism Studies*, 17(6): 763–780.

Jones, N. (2006) *Trading Information: Leaks, Lies and Tip-offs.* London: Politico's Publishing Ltd.

Kenny, K. (2019) *Whistleblowing: Toward a New Theory.* Cambridge, MA: Harvard University Press.

Lashmar, P. (2020) *Spies, Spin and the Fourth Estate: British Intelligence and the Media.* Edinburgh: Edinburgh University Press.

Lévi-Strauss, C. (1978) *Myth and Meaning.* Toronto: University of Toronto Press.

Lewis, J., A. Williams & B. Franklin (2008a) 'A compromised fourth estate? UK journalism, public relations and news sources', *Journalism Studies,* 9(1): 1–20.

Lewis, J., A. Williams & B. Franklin (2008b) 'Four rumours and an explanation', *Journalism Practice,* 2(1): 27–45.

Macnamara, J. (2016) 'The continuing convergence of journalism and PR: new insights for ethical practice from a three-country study of senior practitioners', *Journalism & Mass Communication Quarterly,* 93(1): 118–141.

McChesney, R. W. (2012) 'Farewell to journalism?', *Journalism Studies,* 13(5–6): 682–694.

Malling, M. (2021) 'Reconstructing the informal and invisible: interactions between journalists and political sources in two countries', *Journalism Practice,* doi: 10.1080/17512786.2021.1930571

Marshall, P. D. (2014) *Celebrity and Power: Fame in Contemporary Culture.* Minneapolis: University of Minnesota Press.

Melley, T. (2012) *The Covert Sphere: Secrecy, Fiction, and the National Security State.* Ithaca, New York: Cornell University Press.

Moloney, K. & C. McGrath (2020) *Rethinking Public Relations: Persuasion, Democracy and Society* (3rd ed). London & New York: Routledge.

Munro, I. (2017) 'Whistle-blowing and the politics of truth: Mobilizing "truth games" in the WikiLeaks case', *Human Relations,* 70(5): 519–543.

Norton-Taylor, R. (2020) *The State of Secrecy: Spies and the Media in Britain.* London: I.B. Tauris.

Nuki, P. & B. Gardner (2020) 'Exercise Cygnus uncovered: the pandemic warnings buried by the government; Exercise Cygnus dramatically exposed the gaps in Britain's pandemic response but its "terrifying" findings have yet to be published', *The Telegraph,* 28 March.

Palmer, J. (2000) *Spinning into Control: News Values and Source Strategies.* London & New York: Cologne Leicester University Press.

Pegg, D. (2022) 'UK's freedom of information laws are being undermined, warn journalists', *The Guardian,* 22 April. https://www.theguardian.com/politics/2022/apr/07/uk-foi-transparency-laws-are-being-undermined-warn-journalists. Accessed 6/5/22.

Pegg, D. (2020) 'What was Exercise Cygnus and what did it find? The 2016 simulation of a pandemic found holes in the UK's readiness for such a crisis', *The Guardian,* 7 May. https://www.theguardian.com/world/2020/may/07/what-was-exercise-cygnus-and-what-did-it-find.

Phillips, A. (2010) 'Old sources: new bottles. Journalists and their sources online', in N. Fenton (ed) *New Media, Old News: Journalism and Democracy in a Digital Age.* London: Sage. pp. 87–101.

Plummer, K. (2019) *Narrative Power: The Struggle for Human Value.* Cambridge: Polity Press.

Ricoeur, P. (1981) *Paul Ricoeur, Hermeneutics and the Human Sciences: Essays on Language, Action and Interpretation*, trans., & intro by John B. Thompson (ed). Cambridge: Cambridge University Press.

Sellnow, T. L. & M. W. Seeger (2013) *Theorizing Crisis Communication*, Chichester: Wiley-Blackwell.

Simmel, G. (1906) 'The sociology of secrecy and of secret societies', *American Journal of Sociology*, 11(4): 441–498.

Wahl-Jorgensen, K. & J. Hunt (2012) 'Journalism, accountability and the possibilities for structural critique: A case study of coverage of whistleblowing', *Journalism*, 13(4): 399–416.

Vos, T.P. (ed) (2018) *Journalism.* Boston, MA & Berlin: De Gruyter.

Walby, K. & A. Luscombe (2020) 'Freedom of Information research and cultural studies: a subterranean affinity', *Cultural Studies ↔ Critical Methodologies*, 21(1): 70–79.

Wheatley, D. (2020) 'A typology of news sourcing: routine and non-routine channels of production', *Journalism Practice*, 14(3): 277–298.

Worthy, B. (2017) *The Politics of Freedom of Information.* Manchester: Manchester University Press.

6 Theorising secrecy and the media today

Throughout the book, I have emphasised that practices of both secrecy and publicity are embedded in social practices, social institutions and various forms of legislation and governance rather than existing in some abstract philosophical form. Recognising the specificities of such situatedness facilitates a finely tuned analysis of secrecy and publicity and their wider social impact. This chapter draws together the various analytic strands of my argument and expands its scope to consider the broader significance of secrecy and publicity today.

Has secrecy has become more prevalent today? Framing the question in this way will not produce an unambiguous answer for secrecy exists in a dynamic tension with what Simmel calls (1906) 'publicity' (the making public of information, interests, actions, etc.) and the relative emphasis on, and specific character of each will vary. Instead, we can ask what the relationship between secrecy and publicity *generates* and how that relationship and its impact shift in response to specific power relations and forms of social reciprocity while also influencing them. In parallel, we can widen the analytic lens by asking how the very meanings of secrecy and publicity change over time.

The knowledge of others: news media cultures and social technologies of secrecy

Practices of secrecy and publicity, I have argued, are central constitutive elements of PR and news media cultures. Here, I want to extend this analysis by focusing on Simmel's (1906) interest in the role of social reciprocity and knowledge of others in the secrecy–publicity dynamic. At the core of Simmel's (1906: 441) concept of society is the understanding that social relationships are based on knowledge and reciprocity which are central to fostering the essential element of trust: 'all relationships of people to each other rest, as a matter of course,

DOI: 10.4324/9781003369585-6

upon the precondition that they know something about each other'. In line with his analytic commitment to relationality and interaction, Simmel notes that the forms of social reciprocity, and the modes through which we know others, are socially situated. They vary according to time and place, but also are active in forming and reshaping those social contexts. Reciprocal knowledge functions differently in small communities in which most people know each other personally, compared to large communities such as cities where such knowledge – and trust in others – is mediated through a range of social formations and institutions. In modern societies, Simmel suggests,

> ... life rests upon a thousand presuppositions which the individual can never trace back to their origins, and verify; but which he must accept upon faith and belief. In a much wider degree than people are accustomed to realise, modern civilised life – from the economic system which is constantly becoming more and more a credit-economy, to the pursuit of science, in which the majority of investigators must use countless results obtained by others, and not directly subject to verification – depends upon faith in the honor of others. We rest our most serious decisions upon complicated system of conceptions, the majority of which presuppose confidence that we have not been deceived.
>
> (Simmel 1906: 445–446)

This is the context in which secrecy and deception operate, trading on knowledge of others and knowledge to be withheld from others. In parallel, publicity operates to broadcast information and acts as the mediator of knowledge of others. As discussed in previous chapters, Simmel (1906: 462) argued that secrecy is a great accomplishment of humanity, enabling both individual and social advancement: 'secrecy procures enormous extension of life, because with publicity many sorts of purposes could never arrive at realization'. In this way, secrecy is productive: it not only generates beneficial capacities, it *creates* social relations.

Seen from this perspective, today's news media cultures, and the forms of 'interested communication' such as PR that interface with them, mediate knowledge of others which is central to producing social relationships, social reciprocity and trust, and in this way stitch together 'society'. It is, of course, well understood that news media provide knowledge of others which is crucial for organising societies' understandings, political systems, national identities and distribution of resources (see Chouliaraki 2013; Reese 2021; Schudson 2018). But I am suggesting that approaching the issue through the analysis of secrecy–publicity offers an additional perspective. The secrecy–publicity dynamic is not simply an *effect* of media cultures (whereby the media act to conceal certain issues and publicise others). Instead, we need to appreciate that practices of secrecy and publicity are stitched into the very fabric of social relations within which news media cultures are themselves situated. But following Simmel's analytic principles of relationality and co-constitution, we can understand the relationship between secrecy and news media cultures as fundamentally co-involved. While secrecy seems to be an essential human practice that precedes contemporary news cultures, we can appreciate that news media cultures and cultural industries today provide the primary means through which we access knowledge of others via a range of platforms including social media, broadcast news media and internet sites. Such knowledge of others is central to the constitution of social relations *and* of practices of secrecy–publicity.

While the manifestations of secrecy and publicity vary according to time and place, Simmel's (1906) analysis, alongside a range of others discussed in Chapter 2, suggests that certain key characteristics of secrecy can be tracked consistently: power relations are central to secrecy, shaping the context within which secrecy operates, while secrecy, in turn, shapes the operation of power relations; secrecy practices actively create social relations; secrecy is based on and involves complex forms of social reciprocity. Analysing the particular manifestations of secrecy–publicity can, therefore, reveal much about a specific time and culture and its operations of power, the dominant forms of social reciprocity and the modes through which social relationships are generated, maintained or challenged. As Simmel (1906: 462) argues, 'Every relationship between two individuals or two groups will be characterized by the ratio of secrecy that is involved in it'. But as Foucault (1990) notes, we should not restrict our analysis to asking why particular discursive forms appear or are dominant at any one point in time. Discourses are not simply situated in history; they are productive of those historical contexts. We need to recognise that discourse,

> ... is not an ideal, timeless form that also possesses a history; the problem is not therefore to ask oneself how and why it was able to emerge and become embodied at this point in time; it is, from beginning to end, historical – a fragment of history, a unity

and discontinuity in history itself, posing the problem of its own limits, its divisions, its transformations, the specific modes of its temporality rather than its sudden irruption in the midst of the complicities of time.

(Foucault 2001: 117)

In this sense, the relationship between secrecy and publicity is constitutive of a particular historical moment and shapes our experience and understanding of it. One striking feature of the secrecy–publicity dynamic in many contemporary western societies is its relationship to promotional culture and this impacts powerfully on our experience and understanding of societies today.

The shadow world of the media sphere

Throughout the book, I have explored the creation of a shadow world of the media sphere and analysed its social impact. This shadow world is a constellation of pockets of secrecy – of hidden dimensions – which shift and develop, merge and dissipate. These hidden pockets or dimensions are generated by practices of secrecy and the dynamic interface between secrecy and publicity. I have argued that these pockets of secrecy emerge from the intersection of material and discursive forms such as legislation and regulation (e.g. NDAs, FOI laws), financial and corporate power (exerted through the threat of legal action, monopolies of media ownership, practices of data capture), PR practices of concealment, diversion and publicity and journalists' practices of investigation and revelation. In Chapter 3, I analysed PR's techniques of concealment which I framed in Foucaultian terms as 'technologies of secrecy': distraction and diversion, 'databombing', 'astroturfing' and the creation of counterfeit news stories, preventive revelations and the outweighing of negative issues with positive news coverage.

Such techniques help generate modes of secrecy that actively create social relations by establishing groups privy to certain knowledge (PR's clients) and those excluded from that knowledge (e.g. the public, regulatory bodies). Although these pockets of secrecy are often temporary and fragile – always at risk of exposure – they nevertheless create an obscure space and set of hierarchical relationships that benefit those engaged in such PR practices. This shadow world may have a liminal relationship to what Simmel (1906: 462) calls the 'obvious world', and may operate according to a different timescale and follow different logics, while exerting unseen influence over it. It offers PR's clients a hidden space in which to strategise, 'war game', develop initiatives and consolidate power, all of which ultimately impact upon the obvious world. For instance, PR practices may conceal or diminish instances of malpractice that would damage a company's chances of securing a new contract or attracting investors. They manage the flow of information, and the framing of such information, in a way that disadvantages some (such as the public) and creates an uneven playing field for democratic processes. This shadow world, therefore, acts not only as a container for information obscured by PR, but it shapes its parallel world, the visible media sphere. PR offers clients the benefits of this parallel world composed of emergent and dissipating pockets of secrecy, and also a connection between this shadow world and the 'obvious world' via forms of public engagement which are carefully managed through the range of techniques outlined in Chapter 3. It interfaces with journalists' practices of investigation and revelation as I have explored in Chapters 4 and 5, influencing what enters the realm of 'publicity'.

The social influence of PR has been variously conceived (see Chapter 2), and there has recently been a resurgence in analysing the relationship of PR to propaganda. PR has itself been understood as a form of 'weak propaganda' (Moloney & McGrath 2020: 6), accounts have shown how the practices of PR can merge with those of state propaganda (Briant 2019) and there are ongoing debates about how forms of persuasive communication, such as advertising, PR and propaganda can all involve varying degrees of deception, manipulation, incentivisation and coercion (Bakir et al. 2019). But my account suggests that PR's influence extends beyond shaping opinion and changing minds. Its power is broader, deeper and more subtle: through its management of information and management of access to information, PR actively creates and organises social relations, social reciprocity and power relations.

Transparency as the cure for secrecy?

The solution proposed to the perceived problem of secrecy in both the media sphere and society more generally tends to be transparency (Etzioni 2010). Many organisations lobby for greater transparency in social, political and economic life and offer resources to combat secrecy.[1] Transparency International, for instance, operates an open access database on lobbying which gathers and publicises information about power and influence. For example, it identifies the company/individual which had the most contacts with government ministers for the purposes of lobbying between 2012 and 2022 as BAE

Systems.[2] Equally, one of the most basic premises of journalism is
that uncovering information and contributing to a culture of transparency is a fundamental element of democratic culture, as the journalists and editors in my study all emphasised (see also Reese 2021;
Rusbridger 2019).

But it is widely recognised that transparency measures alone are
inadequate to the task of addressing power differentials and effect-
ing positive change. As I have noted in previous chapters, merely
releasing data or revealing information does not necessarily foster
understanding or facilitate action. In fact, studies have shown how
transparency measures can be mobilised in unintended ways or have
unforeseen consequences. For instance, Bourne (2020) argues that in
business-to-business markets, transparency can function as means of
gaining competitive advantage by enhancing a business' market posi-
tioning. In relation to platforms and data systems, 'making one part of
an algorithmic system visible – such as the algorithm, or even the un-
derlying data – is not the same as holding the assemblage accountable'
(Ananny & Crawford 2018: 984), and the commodification of personal
data is stitched together with practices of transparency in complex
ways (Crain 2018). More fundamentally, the practices associated with
transparency that are intended to foster accountability can paradoxically enhance the efficient functioning of inequitable systems, bolstering techniques of governance while transferring the responsibility for
monitoring and auditing from the state (for instance, through regulation and legislation) to the citizen who is tasked with interrogating
information that is released under principles of transparency (Birchall
2014, 2016). In the context of debates about journalism, Schudson
(2020: 1677) places issues of transparency in a wider context arguing
that, 'transparency is not at the heart of democracy. Accountability is,
and transparency is one, sometimes useful, sometimes devilish, path
to it'. As I explore in the sections below, analysing practices of secrecy
and transparency also highlights broader problems with the organisation of society.

In previous chapters, I have argued that transparency is one manifestation of publicity – perhaps one of the most dominant versions
of publicity today – and, as such, is held in a dynamic tension with
secrecy: as practices of secrecy shift and change, so too will practices
of publicity. But, as I explore in the next section, the very *meanings* and
social traction of both secrecy and publicity may also be shifting. This
raises the intriguing question: what secrets matter today and why do
they matter?

What does secrecy mean today?

Simmel (1906) argued that secrecy practices actively create social relations, organise social reciprocity and structure society. We should also note that changes in social relations, social reciprocity and society impact upon secrecy and how it is practiced. With social change, new forms of social reciprocity develop and new technological affordances create novel social connections, forms of financial appropriation and indeed exploitation. In what follows I signal some important shifts, all of which require detailed research and analysis which is beyond the scope of the present study.

The development of social media is a key factor which reconfigures both the meanings and practices of secrecy alongside its relationship to publicity. Social media offer opportunities for PR communications as well as efficient means for journalists to contact sources and disseminate their news stories. More generally, social media today act as major providers of news (Cairncross 2019; Ofcom 2021), the basis for 'knowledge of others' that is central to social relations. The parameters of tightly controlled corporate or governmental communications can be circumvented by social media which enable new forms of mass circulation and foster widely discussed new forms of 'publicity'. Social media create new forms of social connection and new kinds of communicative reciprocity that tap into and alter the secrecy–publicity dynamic. As Simmel (1906: 466) argues, 'Secrecy sets barriers between men, but at the same time offers the seductive temptation to break through the barriers by gossip or confession. This temptation accompanies the psychical life of the secret like an overtone'. Social media offer a powerful means of circulating 'unofficial news' (first-hand witness reports, rumour, gossip, speculation, etc.) and can facilitate progressive social change, for instance, in coordinating resistance to oppressive regimes or challenging political bias or misinformation. Social media can also amplify the lure or charm of the secrecy–publicity dynamic by whetting public appetite for revelation and, potentially, for forms of positive social change. The shifts in communicative potential represented by social media can change the valences, or socially embedded meanings, of both secrecy and of publicity.

The expansion of data capture and the use of algorithms across a range of fields, including the promotional industries of marketing, advertising and PR, also shifts the meanings and public understandings of secrecy. Vast quantities of data about the public are collected and – despite UK GDPR legislation, and measures to make visible those processes and secure consent from the public – it is not clear that the public is aware of the scale of data collection or how those data are being used (Ofcom 2022). These data collection practices are, in every practical sense, secret and they create secret banks of knowledge to which only select groups and individuals have access. This generates new forms of 'commercial secrets' that may be distinct from the legally protected category of 'trade secrets', and new levels of public ignorance about the operations of knowledge and power (particularly those of large corporations). In parallel, the growth in use of algorithms shifts the meanings and social traction of secrecy by capturing data which reveal patterns about our lives of which we ourselves are unaware. These are secrets about ourselves that are gathered and analysed by automated processes and withheld from us, shifting the terrain of secrecy in new and potentially disturbing ways.

Secrecy's relation to social media and algorithms raises the issue of privacy, particularly in relation to data. Privacy is not identical to secrecy for, as Bok notes, privacy can be seen as...

> ... the condition of being protected from unwanted access by others – either physical access, personal information, or attention. Claims to privacy are claims to control access to what one takes – however grandiosely – to be one's personal domain.... Privacy and secrecy overlap whenever the efforts at such control rely on hiding. But privacy need not hide; and secrecy hides far more than what is private.
>
> (Bok 1989: 10–11)

Privacy is a potent discourse today, mobilising the force of law in protecting some aspects of personal data, but is 'a poor foundation on which to build collective action' as it so in thrall to individualism and thus 'reinforces a sense of self that lives in political isolation' (Birchall 2021: 108–109). But there may be instances when a public concern for privacy may develop into a larger, politically progressive concern about institutional secrecy and power. The UK public seems exercised about a lack of transparency in some areas of public life, such as in political scandals, and concerned about how the public's data may be used, although they may be uncertain about the precise mechanisms (Ofcom 2022), as noted above. Rachel Oldroyd, former Managing Editor and CEO of the Bureau of Investigative Journalism, expresses a view common amongst journalists in my study:

> I think the public care a lot more about privacy than they used to. You know, when the Bureau [of Investigative Journalism]

launched its case [in relation to the Edward] Snowdon [report], [we thought] 'how are we going to get... the importance of this to land? How are we going to get the public to care about this?'.... There was a certain group of people that really got it and really cared but most people didn't. Now, because everybody's using these devices, we're all using WhatsApp and Signal.... I actually think people are starting to understand and care and it's actually less about what the government holds, particularly in this country because we trust our government, you know, we take the Nanny State approach. But since our data is now controlled by Facebook, we've started to really care. And I think that is translating into a 'Facebook bad, got my data', and 'the government's got my data too, should I start to care about that because I'm thinking about that privacy issue?'

(Rachel Oldroyd, former Managing Editor and CEO of the Bureau of Investigative Journalism, participant 36)

It is interesting to speculate whether the public's demand for transparency (in government, in various aspects of public life) and a demand for personal privacy (in terms of control over one's own data) can be seen as a proxy demand for enhanced democratic practices. If public trust in government and in democratic processes is waning (Bauman & Bordoni 2014; Cronin 2018; Norris 2011), can we see those same concerns about political representation and rights expressed instead through demands for transparency? This is an area requiring further research. It may be that perceptions of secrecy relating to the capture and use of the public's data can catalyse broader concerns, channelling and amplifying demands for more fully democratic cultures.

Other social shifts may reframe secrecy's significance and its public profile. The public revelation of issues of social injustice, whether systematic racism and the legacies of slavery and colonialism, or the prevalence of sexual harassment and sexual violence against women and girls, shapes what is popularly understood as 'secret' and what is understood as 'public'. While racism and sexual violence can in no way be understood as being 'secret' in the sense of unknown – very many people have lived with those experiences for decades and many have given voice to those experiences – the systematic nature and material impact of those injustices have not had a major public profile and have often had the status of what Taussig calls 'public secrets': 'that which is generally known, but cannot be articulated' (1999: 5).[3] The public revelation of systematic social injustices can potentially initiate social change; but it may also shift understandings of what constitutes 'secrecy'. This also foregrounds the important point that perceptions of secrecy–publicity, and the ways in which secrecy can operate detrimentally with regard to less powerful groups, are mediated by people's personal experience of inequalities and by the material practices associated with those inequalities, not simply by the media's organisation of the dynamics of revelation and secrecy, as some accounts such as Dean's (2002) may suggest.

What does publicity mean today?

News culture is one of the most significant manifestations of publicity. I have outlined certain key shifts in journalism and news culture with specific reference to practices of secrecy and publicity in Chapters 4 and 5, showing that as investment in independent journalism declines, opportunities for secrecy in society increase. The practices of secrecy that compose the shadow world of the media sphere can offer significant benefits to organisations and individuals wishing to further their agenda without interference or scrutiny. Alongside major changes in media finance and the public's habits of news consumption (Cairncross 2019; Ofcom 2021), journalists are faced with new challenges. Alan Rusbridger, former editor of *The Guardian* newspaper, describes the ways organisations today obstruct media investigations and obscure certain aspects of their practice, for example, through the use of Non-Disclosure Agreements (NDAs), discussed in Chapter 4:

> … almost everybody, whatever kind of corporation they work for, has to sign an NDA and so I think the employers have found lots of ways of just shutting people up… and then the further up the food chain you get, I think organisations like the police are now much more difficult to hold to account, and by the time you get to the security services…. I think we're about to see a slew of laws that will criminalise the reporting of national security.

But alongside the impact of such shifts on the established institutions of news culture, there are significant changes in the practices and meanings of publicity. As investigative journalism struggles, countertrends are emerging such as the growth of open source investigation. This involves accessing freely available information, usually on the internet, in order to investigate issues and events (Camaj 2021; Müller & Wiik 2021). The most high-profile example of open source investigation is the organisation Bellingcat (see Higgins 2021), a loose collective of individuals which investigates issues such as gas attacks in Syria or Russian state propaganda by trawling through a mass of data from various open sources: Google Maps and satellite images, Google Street View, reports from human rights groups, YouTube footage, geolocating videos, video verification, statements on Facebook, photos from Tumblr, social media, reverse image searching, Wikipedia entries, internet message boards. Bellingcat members can devote hours and hours to such searching and cross-referencing in a way that is impossible for traditional journalists on a tight schedule. Bellingcat's practices of investigation and revelation draw in the public as active partners in recording and investigating events through such open source techniques, as its founder Eliot Higgins told me, 'it's something that anyone can do from the comfort of their own home. They can teach themselves'.

> We're sharing more information about stuff and we share information about events that previously would only really be in the remit of... journalists on the ground and it's like there's a CCTV camera in everyone's pocket nowadays. They just have to pull it out and point it at something and that can be extremely revealing about events that are happening... thousands of miles away.
>
> (Eliot Higgins, founder of Bellingcat, participant 34)

Open source investigation techniques change practices of publicity by opening information up through new, non-institutionalised routes. They push the boundaries of what can be known through new practices of revealing secrets that are openly available, although hidden in plain sight, in the mass of data circulating in the media sphere. At the same time, they shift the meanings of secrecy and of publicity by reframing who has the power of revealing secrets through investigation – not trained, institutionally embedded journalists, but any member of the public.

In more general terms, the meaning of 'publicity' today is shaped by the development of promotional culture. It has been widely noted that promotional culture has become increasingly prominent in many societies, shaping economic relations and industry, the media and cultural landscape, democratic practices and modes of politics, power and identity (Davis 2013). Drawing on principles of the market and market competition, promotional culture places great emphasis on brand, image and reputation (see Banet-Weiser 2012; Hardy 2018). In this context, PR gains more traction as a social, economic and political force as it combines an emphasis on promotion – actively advancing clients' interests in a market-based arena – with an emphasis on image and brand, and specifically reputation enhancement (Cronin 2016, 2018).

The case of 'The Russia Report' and the subsequent discussions it elicited illustrate the significance of PR's role in reputation management, often referred to as reputation laundering. The Russia Report,[4] published in July 2020 by the UK Parliament's Intelligence and Security Committee (ISC), described how the United Kingdom had under-estimated the extent of Russia's targeting of the United Kingdom with disinformation campaigns, cyber-attacks, covertly sponsored political advertising campaigns on social media and the PR techniques of 'astroturfing' (creating and circulating fake public opinion) and 'reputation laundering' to promote a more positive image of Russia.[5]

> The UK welcomed Russian money, and few questions – if any – were asked about the provenance of this considerable wealth. It appears that the UK Government at the time held the belief (more perhaps in hope than expectation) that developing links with major Russian companies would promote good governance by encouraging ethical and transparent practices, and the adoption of a law-based commercial environment. What is now clear is that it was in fact counter-productive, in that it offered ideal mechanisms by which illicit finance could be recycled through what has been referred to as the London 'laundromat'. The money was also invested in extending patronage and building influence across a wide sphere of the British establishment – PR firms, charities, political interests, academia and cultural institutions were all willing beneficiaries of Russian money, contributing to a 'reputation laundering' process. In brief, Russian influence in the UK is 'the new normal', and there are a lot of Russians with very close links to Putin who are well integrated into the UK business and social scene, and accepted because of their wealth. This level of integration – in 'Londongrad' in particular – means that any measures now being taken by the Government are not preventative but rather constitute damage limitation... the arrival of Russian money resulted in a growth industry of enablers – individuals and organisations who manage and lobby for the Russian elite in the UK. Lawyers, accountants, estate agents and PR professionals have played a role, wittingly or unwittingly, in the extension of Russian influence which is often linked to promoting the nefarious interests of the Russian state.
>
> (Intelligence and Security Committee 2020: 15)

The concerns raised in the report were not addressed by the UK government at the time, a failure which looks increasingly short-sighted in the light of Russia's 2022 invasion of Ukraine which highlighted the extent of Russia's financial power and more general influence in the United Kingdom. In fact, it is reported that the UK Prime Minister at the time, Boris Johnson, delayed the publication of the Russia Report, presumably to manage any negative reputational impact on the Conservative Party following revelations about Russian funding and lobbying in the United Kingdom. Following its publication in 2020, the detail and implications of the Russia Report were the subject of further discussion. Former MI6 officer Christopher Steele argued that the United Kingdom requires new legislation to protect it from the influence of foreign powers such as Russia and China: 'When you talk about foreign agents in this instance you are not talking about people who are committing treason or selling secrets to the Russians or the Chinese. You are talking about their agents, in the sense of people who are pursuing their agenda in the UK for money', which, he states, includes PR agencies, lobbyists, law firms and private intelligence companies.[6]

Such practices of managing reputation, by emphasising the positive while concealing the negative (as discussed in Chapter 3), have intensified in the context of promotional culture. But at the same time, corporate or governmental reputation has become more easily contested and hence more fragile. This is due in part to the affordances of digital media – social media enable the public to speak back to organisations and governments and circulate critiques in new ways (Couldry & Hepp 2016). But the fragility of reputation today in the United Kingdom and elsewhere also derives from the public's lack of trust in institutions and their communications (see Phillips 2015; Shilling & Mellor 2015). Hence, it is easy for the public to imagine that society is awash with secrets, and the public may speculatively populate the world with hidden motivations, interests and actions which themselves may fuel conspiracy thinking (see Butter & Knight 2020). As a result, the public may become suspicious of 'reputation', perceiving it as a veneer behind which damning secrets lie. There is, of course, considerable evidence that many damning secrets do, indeed, lie behind brand image and reputational veneer, as Michaels' (2020) work on product defence companies demonstrates (see Chapter 3). Such revelations may in turn sustain and amplify the secrecy–publicity dynamic, and the fragility of reputation itself creates more opportunity for the PR industry to pitch its talents to clients wishing to burnish their image. What publicity means in this context of suspicion and promotionalism may be shifting in ways that are not yet clear but which may have significant social and political impact.

More broadly, as I argued in Chapter 3, PR practices of concealing certain information and intensively promoting other information
skews public understandings of society and how it operates. The combined effect of a PR culture in the news media, alongside the decline
in investment in independent journalism, means that PR hampers
'joined up thinking' about society and how its systems and organisations function. In effect, this creates social relations based on inequitable access to information *and* the tools to analyse it: the information
that is publicised through various communication practices is not
framed in such a way to enable systematic understanding of society.
Such forms of publicity are far removed from the ideal of the public
sphere that Habermas (1991) proposed and represent a disenfranchise-
ment of the public that has far-reaching consequences.

The charm of the secret: social reciprocity and the making of social relations

Secrecy is fascinating: it acts as a lure, compelling investigation and
revelation. The magnetic appeal of the secret that is amplified in the
media can propel the public to search for ever more secrets, as in
Dean's (2002) account. Dean suggests that this is politically paralysing as action is forever deferred in favour of more investigation. But,
I suggest, secrecy's appeal can also act as a focal point for demands
relating to democracy and social justice – in effect, demands for new
forms of social reciprocity and social relations. The following example
is intended to explore the potential of the 'charm of secrecy' (Simmel
1906: 465) to function as a catalyst for social change.

The Guardian newspaper engaged in a detailed investigation called
'The Queen's Consent' relating to the UK monarchy's secretive interference in legislative procedures. The journalists' investigation
produced a series of articles published from 2021. An article entitled,
'Royals vetted more than 1,000 laws via Queen's consent. Exclusive: secretive procedure used to review laws ranging from Brexit trade deal to
inheritance and land policy' outlined the findings of that investigation:

> More than 1,000 laws have been vetted by the Queen or Prince
> Charles through a secretive procedure before they were approved
> by the UK's elected members of parliament, the Guardian has es-
> tablished. The huge number of laws subject to royal vetting cover
> matters ranging from justice, social security, pensions, race re-
> lations and food policy through to obscure rules on car parking
> charges and hovercraft. They included draft laws that affected the

Queen's personal property such as her private estates in Balmoral and Sandringham, and potentially anything deemed to affect her personally.... As part of a series investigating the use of the consent procedure, the Guardian has published documents from the National Archives that reveal the Queen has on occasions used the procedure to privately lobby the government. The investigation uncovered evidence suggesting that she used the procedure to persuade government ministers to change a 1970s transparency law in order to conceal her private wealth from the public.... The database of 1,062 laws relates to legislation that the Queen vetted under consent rules, and it is not known on which occasions she also lobbied for changes to draft legislation. The Guardian has uncovered evidence of lobbying for changes to at least four draft laws, but it is possible she interfered with many more.... Some of the bills the Queen reviewed before they were passed by parliament relate to wealth or taxation. One of the richest families in Britain, with the monarch's property investments exempt from inheritance tax and collections of fine art and jewellery built up over centuries, the Windsors are notoriously guarded about their finances. Members of the Windsor family can have their will sealed from the public, unlike any other family in Britain, ensuring an unmatched level of secrecy around their private wealth.... In 2014, for example, the Queen and the heir to the throne screened the inheritance and trustees' powers bill. Two years earlier she vetted the trusts (capital and income) bill. Trusts are legal arrangements often used by wealthy families to protect their assets from both tax and public scrutiny.[7]

The Guardian's exposé revealed previously unknown details relating to the monarchy's secretive exercise of power. This mode of revelation of controversial issues taps into the lure or charm of the secret, engaging the dynamic tension of the secrecy–publicity relationship, encouraging the public to imagine what else may be concealed and what more may be exposed. *The Guardian's* strategy of releasing the investigation's findings incrementally over a period of months – presumably to keep the issue live in the public mind – bolsters this dynamic. But the veil of secrecy that the monarchy tries to maintain over its practices does not simply trigger journalistic and public curiosity about the nature of the secret. Secrecy here acts as a point of traction for challenging established social structures and social relations, and the UK monarchy's influence and image are nothing if not well-established and protected (see Clancy 2021). *The Guardian* used its investigation to question the legitimacy of the monarchy and its place in a modern democracy:

> The Queen does not meddle in the affairs of parliament. That is a cornerstone of Britain's system of constitutional monarchy. Or at least it is supposed to be. The Guardian's investigation into the secretive power of Queen's consent, whereby the monarch is provided with advance sight of draft laws and invited to approve them, casts this fundamental assumption into doubt.[8]

Here, the media are feeding a public fascination for revelation of secrets. But they are also revealing the obscure operation of power relations, how those power relations constitute social relations and society more generally and how specific forms of social reciprocity are stitched together with secrecy. The media provide the 'knowledge of others' that Simmel (1906) argues is central to the creation of social relations. At the same time, they are fostering the possibility of social change and new modes of social reciprocity, in this case, dispensing with the deference traditionally accorded to the monarchy as an acknowledgement of social status and challenging the legitimacy of the very institution of the monarchy and its conventional place in the social hierarchy. Here, the charm of secrecy is both a magnetic appeal and a form of social magic – a lever that has the potential to effect social change. As Foucault argues, power intersects with knowledge in a shifting dynamic which then acts as a form of transformational matrix: 'Relations of power–knowledge are not static forms of distribution, they are "matrices of transformations"' (1990: 99). The powers of revelation, and the lure of secrecy, can thus act to initiate social transformations in ways that may be unpredictable and profound.

What secrets matter and why?

The power of secrecy derives partly from its capacity to manage public perceptions of *what matters*: what issues should be placed on the public agenda for scrutiny and potential action. Journalism is tasked with the framing of news reports in such ways that engage the public and expand the public's understanding of what merits their attention. As journalist Roy Greenslade suggests, an inherent difficulty in investigative reporting is the misalignment of its practices and orientation with public expectations and concerns:

> It's a whole messy business revealing secrets and revealing things people want to know. I think the difficulty is there's a mismatch

between what people think the media should be doing and what the media do and I don't think that there's a really easy answer to explaining that. We do this for you, but you don't care that we do it for you.

(Roy Greenslade, participant 20)

Framing news reports to show the public why they should care is a core function of journalism:

… the point of journalism is to find those things out and explain to the public why they need to care about it, and the job of the journalist is to say there's something going on here you don't know about, or you may not think you need to know about, but here's why it matters to you.

(Rachel Oldroyd, former Managing Editor & CEO of the Bureau of Investigative Journalism, participant 36)

As the Cairncross Review found, 'the stories people want to read may not always be the ones that they ought to read in order to ensure that a democracy can hold its public servants properly to account' (Cairncross 2019: 102). Independent journalism's agenda of publicity, therefore, may be in tension with secrecy's practices of preventing certain issues' appearance on the public agenda by keeping them out of the media sphere – a dynamic that the public may not be in a position to recognise. Nevertheless, exposés of secrets and secret interests may function as powerful means not only to initiate social change, but to convince the public that independent journalism matters and should be supported.

Secrecy also comes to matter particularly intensely when it becomes a constitutive element of an organisation's or institution's culture. Many journalists' accounts have noted the insidious effect of 'cultures of secrecy' in government, whereby attempts are made to suppress stories, divert public attention and discredit journalists (Lashmar 2020; Norton-Taylor 2020). This theme emerged strongly in my interviews with journalists and editors who discussed their experiences of investigating powerful organisations, whether governments or large corporations, which wish to shield themselves from public scrutiny or the demands of transparency. As an investigative journalist at a national UK newspaper described:

One of the biggest problems afflicting government is a kind of culture of secrecy. It's not that they want to keep things secret, it's just that instinctively they keep things secret because they haven't thought of a reason why they shouldn't and it can often lead them down paths of behaviour and action that are entirely pointless and result in them wasting a great deal of time trying to keep something secret as though it's very sensitive when actually it's not.... I think there is a kind of secrecy disease that afflicts government where stuff is just kept secret for irrational reasons where it's not because they've decided that they want to keep it secret, it's just because secrecy is the default.

(participant 33)

Many organisations' default position is that of withholding information without compelling reason. This can be illustrated in comments by Gary Younge, former investigative journalist, when discussing his reporting of UK knife crime figures:

It was not public knowledge how many kids each year had been killed by knives, which was amazing given how much ink had been spilled over knife crime, and [the government] wouldn't tell us, so we filed a bunch of FOI [Freedom of Information] requests and eventually got the numbers, which told a very different story to the national narrative in terms of race and place, and gender actually, and I had no idea why they wouldn't release those figures.... So, I've seen an awful lot of secrecy when I've not really understood why, what the secrecy was for.

(Gary Younge, participant 22)

While clearly making journalists' task more challenging, the cultures of secrecy that have developed in some organisations and institutions also function to create social relations. They act to make a particular organisation cohere as an entity, firming its boundaries and shaping its core practices (Costas & Grey 2016), while establishing social relations based on principles of restriction and exclusion. As Lashmar (2020) notes, such cultures of secrecy in government have inhibited informed public debate about democracy while encouraging institutional complacency which may have hampered the government's ability to recognise emerging new threats.

In theorising secrecy and its relationship to transparency, some authors have attempted to dislodge the dualism of secrecy–publicity. Gilbert (2007: 38) suggests we dispense with the standard societal response to secrecy–publicity and the way in which transparency and disclosure are posited as the opposite of, and solution to, secrecy: 'This is not to say that democratic politics can ever do *without* gestures of disclosure, but it requires that those gestures at least sometime go beyond the mere telling of secrets and become real acts of what we might call, idiosyncratically, "publication", or "publicity'". This is suggestive of an ideal public sphere in which publicity provides the foundation for a truly democratic society. Similarly, Birchall (2021: 176) argues for 'postsecrecy' which involves an 'understanding and experience of the political that is free from the false choice between secrecy and transparency as these terms are commonly understood and enacted today'. Birchall (2021), alongside others, makes the strong point that we should challenge the assumption that transparency and revelation will resolve problems with democracy.

Such approaches to secrecy, I would suggest, are, in fact, calling for a new politics and a new form of democracy. This is a perspective for which I have sympathy and there are many accounts which explore what forms such a politics and democracy may take (for example, Butler 2018; Fraser & Jaeggi 2018). Secrecy may be understood, as in Simmel's (1906) account, as a foundational human characteristic that shapes social relations. As it also structures power relations and hierarchies, I suggest that we can also understand manifestations of secrecy as symptoms of problems in society. The secrecy practices of corporations, governments or other bodies, as in the example of the UK monarchy above, signal wider problems with democratic practices and representation, distribution of resources and power differentials. Secrecy can be found in many of the most problematic social practices today: off-shore finance; corporate political lobbying; institutionalised nepotism; environmentally destructive products and practices; data capture, exploitation and surveillance; hidden vested interests; mass scale money laundering; covert illegal state practices. Attempting to challenge the secrecy that is evident in such practices will not address the more fundamental issues of power and influence that lie behind them – these would, no doubt, find expression in other ways should the tool of secrecy no longer be available.

But while we reimagine such new forms of politics and democracy it will be necessary to live with and address the practices of secrecy and publicity which currently have a constitutive role in many societies. I have argued that rather than simply paralysing action or bolstering an unproductive and constraining dualism of secrecy–publicity, practices of revelation can offer radical potential for social action and social change. As Foucault argues,

> A discursive formation does not occupy therefore all the possible volume that is opened up to it of right by the systems of formation

of its objects, its enunciations, and its concepts; it is essentially incomplete, owing to the system of formation of its strategic choices. Hence the fact that, taken up again, placed, and interpreted in a new constellation, a given discursive formation may reveal new possibilities...

(Foucault 2001: 67)

Framed in this way, we can appreciate that practices of secrecy–publicity do not necessarily constitute a closed system: they can open up lines of possibility that extend beyond the current parameters of neoliberal consumer capitalism and compromised democratic processes. Addressing today's problematic practices of secrecy and mobilising principles of transparency – oriented, crucially, towards the need for greater *accountability* – may advance the broader project of shifting societal formations.

I have emphasised that PR has become an increasingly powerful actor, tapping into and shaping a promotional culture that is an important central feature of neoliberal capitalism: PR's emphasis on image and reputation functions as a key tool for the operation of markets based on distinction and competition. Understanding PR today will, therefore, provide insights into how capitalism operates and how it may be shifting. PR also acts to shape powerful manifestations of both secrecy and publicity, impacting on news culture and creating a shadow world of the media sphere. Alongside organising practices of camouflage, misdirection and reputational management, PR also conceals its own operation from the public and mitigates against a systematic appreciation of capitalism's processes and institutions. This is not a conspiracy in which PR agencies and practitioners collaborate in order to obscure how the social world operates, but the aggregated impact of dispersed, interest-driven communications of corporations, individuals, institutions and governments which offer partial and disconnected informational outputs. Analysing PR's role in shaping such a terrain of secrecy and publicity brings us some way towards understanding contemporary operations of power and towards reimagining what other social relations may be possible.

Notes

1 For example, see They Work for You https://www.theyworkforyou.com/; My Little Crony https://www.sophie-e-hill.com/slides/my-little-crony/; Corporate Watch https://corporatewatch.org/; What Do They Know? https://www.whatdotheyknow.com/; open Democracy https://www.open-democracy.net/en/.

2 https://openaccess.transparency.org.uk/. Accessed 10/5/22.
3 This also references the hidden nature of 'domestic' violence and what occurs in the 'private sphere'.
4 Intelligence and Security Committee (2020) 'Russia'. HC 632 – Intelligence and Security Committee of Parliament – Russia (independent.gov.uk) Accessed 23/3/22. Several sections of the report were redacted before publication for reasons of security.
5 The Russia Report's (2020: 1) comments on Russia's threat to world order, published before Russia's mass invasion of Ukraine in 2022, are intriguing: 'The security threat posed by Russia is difficult for the West to manage as, in our view and that of many others, it appears fundamentally nihilistic. Russia seems to see foreign policy as a zero-sum game: any actions it can take which damage the West are fundamentally good for Russia. It is also seemingly fed by paranoia, believing that Western institutions such as NATO and the EU have a far more aggressive posture towards it than they do in reality. There is also a sense that Russia believes that an undemocratic "might is right" world order plays to its strengths, which leads it to seek to undermine the Rules Based International Order – whilst nonetheless benefitting from its membership of international political and economic institutions'.
6 Gordon Corera, 'Christopher Steele: Urgent need for laws to stop foreign influence' https://www.bbc.co.uk/news/uk-56348936. Accessed 11/3/21.
7 https://www.theguardian.com/uk-news/2021/feb/08/royals-vetted-more-than-1000-laws-via-queens-consent. Accessed 9/2/21. David Pegg, Rob Evans and Michael Barton 'Royals vetted more than 1,000 laws via Queen's consent. Exclusive: secretive procedure used to review laws ranging from Brexit trade deal to inheritance and land policy'. *The Guardian.* Monday 8 February 2021.
8 https://www.theguardian.com/uk-news/2021/feb/07/how-queens-consent-raises-questions-over-uk-democracy. Accessed 7/2/21. David Pegg and Rob Evans, 'How Queen's consent raises questions over UK democracy: The monarch is not supposed to meddle in parliament. But that key principle is now in doubt'. *The Guardian.* Sunday 7 February 2021.

References

Ananny, M. & K. Crawford (2018) 'Seeing without knowing: limitations of the transparency ideal and its application to algorithmic accountability', *New Media & Society*, 20(3): 973–989.

Bakir, V., E. Herring, D. Miller & P. Robinson (2019) 'Organised persuasive communication: a new conceptual framework for research on public relations, propaganda and promotional culture', *Critical Sociology*, 45(3): 311–328.

Banet-Weiser, S. (2012) *Authentic™: The Politics of Ambivalence in a Brand Culture*. New York: New York University Press.

Bauman, Z. & C. Bordoni (2014) *State of Crisis*. Cambridge, MA: Polity.

Birchall, C. (2021) *Radical Secrecy: The Ends of Transparency in Datafied America*. Minneapolis, MN: University of Minnesota Press.

Birchall, C. (2016) 'Managing secrecy', *International Journal of Communication*, 10: 152–163.

Birchall, C. (2014) 'Radical transparency?', *Cultural Studies ↔ Critical Methodologies*, 14(1): 77–88.

Bok, S. (1989) *Secrets: On the Ethics of Concealment and Revelation*. New York: Vintage Books.

Bourne, C. (2020) 'Fintech's transparency–publicity nexus: value cocreation through transparency discourses in business-to-business digital marketing', *American Behavioral Scientist*, 64(11): 1607–1626.

Briant, E. L. (2019) 'Pentagon Ju-Jitsu – reshaping the field of propaganda', *Critical Sociology*, 45(3): 361–378.

Butler, J. (2018) *Notes Towards a Performative Theory of Assembly*. Cambridge, MA: Harvard University Press.

Butter, M. & P. Knight (eds) (2020) *Routledge Handbook of Conspiracy Theories*. London & New York: Routledge.

Cairncross, F. (2019) *The Cairncross Review: A Sustainable Future for Journalism*. https://assets.publishing.service.gov.uk/government/uploads/system/uploads/attachment_data/file/779882/021919_DCMS_Cairncross_Review_.pdf. Accessed 19/4/22

Camaj, L. (2021) 'The monitorial role of crowdsourced journalism: audience engagement in corruption reporting in nonprofit newsrooms', *Journalism Practice*. https://doi.org/10.1080/17512786.2021.1960587

Chouliaraki, L. (2013) *The Ironic Spectator: Solidarity in the Age of Posthumanitarianism*. Cambridge, MA: Polity.

Clancy, L. (2021) *Running the Family Firm: How the Monarchy Manages Its Image and Our Money*. Manchester: Manchester University Press.

Costas, J. & C. Grey (2016) *Secrecy at Work: The Hidden Architecture of Organizational Life*. Stanford: Stanford University Press.

Couldry, N. & A. Hepp (2016) *The Mediated Construction of Reality*. Cambridge, MA: Polity.

Crain, M. (2018) 'The limits of transparency: data brokers and commodification', *New Media & Society*, 20(1): 88–104.

Cronin, A. M. (2018) *Public Relations Capitalism: Promotional Culture, Publics and Commercial Democracy*. Basingstoke: Palgrave Macmillan.

Cronin, A.M. (2016) 'Reputational capital in "the PR University": public relations and market rationalities', *Journal of Cultural Economy*, 9(4): 396–409.

Davis, A. (2013) *Promotional Cultures: The Rise and Spread of Advertising, Public Relations, Marketing and Branding*. Cambridge, MA: Polity Press.

Dean, J. (2002) *Publicity's Secret: How Technoculture Capitalizes on Democracy*. New York: Cornell University Press.

Etzioni, A. (2010) 'Is transparency the best disinfectant?', *The Journal of Political Philosophy* 18(4): 389–404.

Foucault, M. (2001) *The Archaeology of Knowledge*, trans. S. Smith. London: Routledge.

Foucault, M. (1990) *The History of Sexuality, Volume 1*, trans. Robert Hurley. London: Penguin.

Fraser, N. & R. Jaeggi (2018) *Capitalism: A Conversation in Critical Theory.* B. Milstein (ed). Cambridge, MA: Polity.

Gilbert, J. (2007) 'Public secrets: "Being-with" in an era of perpetual disclosure', *Cultural Studies*, 21(1): 22–41.

Habermas, J. (1991) *The Structural Transformation of the Public Sphere.* Cambridge, MA: MIT Press.

Hardy, J. (2018) *Branded Content: The Fateful Merging of Media and Marketing.* Abingdon: Routledge.

Higgins, E. (2021) *We Are Bellingcat: An Intelligence Agency for the People.* London: Bloomsbury.

Lashmar, P. (2020) *Spies, Spin and the Fourth Estate: British Intelligence and the Media.* Edinburgh: Edinburgh University Press.

Michaels, D. (2020) *The Triumph of Doubt: Dark Money and the Science of Deception*, Oxford & New York: Oxford University Press.

Moloney, K. & C. McGrath (2020) *Rethinking Public Relations: Persuasion, Democracy and Society* (3rd ed). London: Routledge.

Müller, N. C. & J. Wiik (2021) 'From gatekeeper to gate-opener: open-source spaces in investigative journalism', *Journalism Practice*. https://doi.org/10.1 080/17512786.2021.1919543

Norris, P. (2011) *Democratic Deficit: Critical Citizens Revisited.* Cambridge: Cambridge University Press.

Norton-Taylor, R. (2020) *The State of Secrecy: Spies and the Media in Britain.* London: I.B. Tauris.

Ofcom (2022) *Adults' Media Use and Attitudes Report.* https://www.ofcom.org. uk/__data/assets/pdf_file/0020/234362/adults-media-use-and-attitudes-report-2022.pdf. Accessed 14/7/22.

Ofcom (2021) *News Consumption in the UK: 2021.* https://www.ofcom.org. uk/__data/assets/pdf_file/0025/222478/news-consumption-in-the-uk-overview-of-findings-2021.pdf. Accessed 16/6/22.

Phillips, R. (2015) *Trust Me, PR Is Dead.* London: Unbound.

Reese, S. D. (2021) *The Crisis of the Institutional Press.* Cambridge, MA: Polity.

Rusbridger, A. (2019) *Breaking News: The Remaking of Journalism and Why It Matters Now.* Edinburgh: Canongate.

Schudson, M. (2020) 'The shortcomings of transparency for democracy', *American Behavioral Scientist*, 64(11): 1670–1678.

Schudson, M. (2018) *Why Journalism Still Matters.* Cambridge, MA: Polity Press.

Shilling, C. & P. A. Mellor (2015) 'For a sociology of deceit: doubled identities, interested actions and situational logics of opportunity', *Sociology*, 49(4): 607–623.

Simmel, G. (1906) 'The sociology of secrecy and of secret societies', *American Journal of Sociology*, 11(4): 441–498.

Taussig, M. (1999) *Defacement: Public Secrecy and the Labor of the Negative.* Stanford: Stanford University Press.

Index

For Product Safety Concerns and Information please contact our EU
representative GPSR@taylorandfrancis.com
Taylor & Francis Verlag GmbH, Kaufingerstraße 24, 80331 München, Germany